THE First Ladies

THE First Ladies

THEIR LIVES AND LEGACIES

DEBORAH JONES SHERWOOD

BARNES
&NOBLE
BOOKS
NEW YORK

A BARNES & NOBLE BOOK

Library of Congress Cataloging-in-Publication Data

Sherwood, Deborah Jones.
  The first ladies: their lives and legacies / by Deborah Jones Sherwood.
    p. cm.
  ISBN 0-7607-4494-7 (alk. paper)
  1. Presidents' spouses—United States—Biography. 2. Presidents'
spouses—United States—History—Chronology. 3. White House
(Washington, D.C.)—History. I. Title.

  E176.2.S54 2003
  973'.09'9--dc21

                                                2003007078

Editor: Hallie Einhorn
Art Director: Kevin Ullrich
Designer: Orit Mardkha-Tenzer
Photography Editor: Chris Bain
Photography Researcher: Melissa McKoy
Production Manager: Michael Vagnetti
Digital Imaging: Daniel J. Rutkowski

Color separations by Bright Arts Graphics (Singapore)
Printed and bound in Singapore by KHL

1 3 5 7 9 10 8 6 4 2

DEDICATION

With love and appreciation to

Dick Motta

Tom Sherwood

and Carl Chamberlain

CONTENTS

INTRODUCTION

"I'd come to realize more clearly the power of the woman in the White House. Not my power, but the power of the position. A power which could be used to help."

—Betty Ford

If a thousand people were to be surveyed with the question "What do you think America's first lady should be like?" there would be a thousand widely different answers. Like the American population itself, the women we have known as our nation's hostesses are an incredibly diverse group. Unavoidably in the limelight, the ladies who preside over the White House become a significant part of our country's history.

From the beginning, one of the basic duties of the first lady has been to serve as hostess for visiting heads of state and other dignitaries. However, the manner in which presidential wives have entertained has differed dramatically. Martha Washington was faced with the challenge of establishing a style that would not be associated with the British royal court, but would command respect nonetheless. From that point on, each woman brought her own individual style to the position. Some, such as Elizabeth Monroe, set a

highly formal tone, while others, such as Lady Bird Johnson, offered a down-home familiarity.

Beyond the obligation to serve as hostess, the largely undefined role of first lady has been left up to the interpretation of the women who have held the position. Many have used their station to call attention to national issues and social causes. In the early 1900s, Ellen Wilson tried to improve (albeit unsuccessfully) living conditions for impoverished residents of the nation's capital. Half a century later, Lady Bird Johnson, a strong advocate for the environment, convinced her husband and Congress to pass the Highway Beautification Act. Hillary Clinton prompted discussion of national health care reform and now serves as a member of the United States Senate.

A number of first ladies have chosen to lead by example. During World War I, Edith Wilson made clothes for soldiers and volunteered at the canteens, where she handed out coffee and

sandwiches. Half a century later, Betty Ford's candidness about her mastectomy led women all across the country to get breast exams. In 1989, Barbara Bush transformed our national awareness of AIDS by inviting the press to photograph her holding an HIV-positive infant.

Throughout America's history—not only in recent years—various first ladies have acted as political advisors to their husbands. Abigail Adams read over her husband's speeches and frequently offered her opinions. In 1919, when Woodrow Wilson suffered from a stroke, Edith Wilson became the literal power behind the president. Rosalynn Carter scheduled weekly working lunches during which she and her husband would discuss political issues. And in 1992, during Bill Clinton's campaign for the presidency, Hillary was

billed as a full partner. Some ambitious women—such as Julia Grant, Helen Taft, and Florence Harding—were the ones who pushed their husbands into office in the first place.

Sometimes the public's response to the influence of these nonelected women has been less than favorable. Eleanor Roosevelt—who traveled extensively on behalf of her husband, reporting back to him on the conditions and programs she had observed—received letters saying she should spend more time with her family. Betty Ford and Hillary Clinton were criticized for their outspokenness and activism.

While there have been many forceful personalities in the role of first lady, there have been some shrinking violets as well. Some presidential wives lived in the background for reasons that ranged

ABOVE: *The first of America's first ladies, Martha Washington demonstrated tact, diplomacy, and a warm sense of hospitality. This piece of art entitled* **The Republican Court** *(also known as* **Lady Washington's Reception***) was painted by Daniel Huntington in 1861.*

BELOW: *Eleanor Roosevelt traveled around the nation to observe the conditions in which people lived and worked; she would then speak with her husband about what she had seen. In May 1935, she visited a coal mine in Ohio to see for herself the environment in which the miners labored.*

OPPOSITE: *The fashions donned by first ladies have long garnered much attention. Jacqueline Kennedy designed and wore this dress for the inaugural ball in 1961. Featuring silk chiffon over peau d'ange, the off-white gown boasts a strapless bodice embellished with silver thread and brilliants. The dress was made by Ethel Frankau of Bergdorf Goodman in New York City.*

from declining health, as was the case with Eliza Johnson and Letitia Tyler, to overriding grief, such as that experienced by Jane Pierce. Others simply had a quietness of character, such as Bess Truman. Many, including Louisa Adams, performed the role admirably but without fanfare.

Many presidential wives have needed to juggle their endeavors as first lady with the responsibilities of motherhood. And raising children in the fishbowl of the White House has never been an easy task. Frances Cleveland was horrified to see her young daughter, "Baby Ruth," being passed around by admirers; she promptly ordered the White House gates closed. Understanding the public's desire to know more about her children but seeking to establish some control, Edith Roosevelt staged photo sessions and had the images released to the press. Jacqueline Kennedy went to great lengths to protect her children's privacy, both during her time in the White House and afterward.

Too often, the legacies that America's first ladies have left us go unattributed. These diverse women have been responsible for a surprising list of significant acts of legislation, not to mention

their behind-the-scenes influence as confidante to one of the most powerful leaders in the world. We have a number of first ladies to thank for the preservation of the White House and a host of other historical treasures. On a smaller scale, first ladies are directly responsible for such simple pleasures as the cherry blossoms that bloom in Washington, D.C., every spring.

This volume explores the numerous contributions that first ladies have made to the nation and the ways in which they have expanded the boundaries of the position itself. The wives of Thomas Jefferson (Martha Wayles Skelton), Andrew Jackson (Rachel Donelson), Martin Van Buren (Hannah Hoes), and Chester Arthur (Ellen Lewis Herndon) are not profiled in this book, as they died before their husbands became president. In the absence of a spouse, each of these men relied upon a number of different women—from female relatives to wives of cabinet members—to fulfill the duties of hostess when necessary. Unfortunately, no complete list of these women exists. With the exception of Dolley Madison—who after acting as the nation's hostess under Thomas Jefferson went on to become first lady when her husband was

elected to the presidency—these women are not profiled because they did not have a continuous presence in the White House, stepping in only as needed. Angelica Singleton Van Buren, however, is discussed because, after her marriage to Abraham Van Buren (son of Martin Van Buren), she became a permanent fixture in the Executive Mansion, fulfilling the role of first lady to the same degree as many presidential wives—even more so than some. Though not married to a president, Harriet Lane is also profiled, as she served as first lady throughout the term of her uncle James Buchanan. Even married presidents sometimes needed to call upon other women to step in as hostess, because the spouse's ailing condition prevented her from carrying out the duty herself. Interestingly, Mrs. Jefferson Davis, who would later become first lady of the Confederacy, served as a substitute hostess for Presidents Taylor, Fillmore, and Pierce prior to the Civil War.

Before proceeding to the profiles within this book, one brief note regarding terminology merits addressing. From the beginning, the structure located at 1600 Pennsylvania Avenue in Washington, D.C., has been known as "the President's House," "the Presidential Palace," "the Executive Mansion," and "the White House." The latter comes from the fact that the sandstone building has always been dressed with whitewash or white paint. Because referring to the presidential home as "the White House" was so common, President Theodore Roosevelt made this the building's official title in 1901.

The following pages bring to light the stories of America's first ladies, focusing on the roles that these prominent women played during their time in the White House. Some first ladies retreated from the responsibility. Others embraced it. None ignored it, nor have we ignored them.

MARTHA DANDRIDGE CUSTIS WASHINGTON

June 2, 1731–May 22, 1802
George Washington, president 1789–1797

"I live a very dull life here [in New York] and know nothing that passes

in the town. I never go to any public place….indeed, I think I am more like

a state prisoner than anything else. There is [sic] certain bounds set for me

which I must not depart from…and as I cannot do as I like,

I am obstinate, and stay at home a great deal."

—Martha Washington in a letter to her niece Frances Washington, October 23, 1789

Martha Dandridge, daughter of Frances Jones and John Dandridge, was born into affluence near Williamsburg, Virginia, in 1731. Her education, which was typical for an eighteenth-century young lady of her social status, covered domestic arts, social skills, and basic reading and math. In 1749, she married Daniel Parke Custis, a wealthy planter almost twice her age. Only eight years later Custis died, leaving Martha with two young children, seventeen thousand acres (6,800ha) of land, hundreds of slaves, and a large fortune; she was the richest widow in the colonies.

In 1758, while visiting friends, Martha was introduced to George Washington, the twenty-six-year-old commander of the Virginia militia. The couple exchanged wedding vows on January 6, 1759. Martha brought additional property, wealth, and social prominence to the marriage—advantages that helped her husband to advance both militarily and politically.

Out of respect to the family of Martha's first husband, George Washington did not adopt Martha's children, but he was a loving and indulgent stepfather. In 1773, at the age of sixteen, Martha's daughter, Patsy, died of epilepsy. Years later, during the American Revolution (1775–1783), Martha's son John Parke Custis, known as Jackie, died of dysentery, which he contracted while serving as an aide to General Washington.

In 1774, as tension increased between the colonies and Great Britain, George Washington was chosen as one of Virginia's delegates to the First Continental Congress. A year later, he was elected commander in chief of the Continental army. During the Revolutionary War, Martha stayed with her husband at the winter encampments, enduring even the severe winter of 1777–1778 at Valley Forge. It was not unusual for wives to travel with their husbands to the camps, where the women were paid to cook, launder, and sometimes nurse the soldiers. Martha encouraged and aided the patriots who were fighting for their lives and their freedom by tending the wounded, writing letters to their loved ones at home, sewing clothing, and giving them provisions from her own home. She also led knitting circles with other camp wives. When Martha was not at the encampments, she supervised the Mount Vernon plantation.

After the war ended, George and Martha settled into a peaceful life at their Mount Vernon estate on the banks of the Potomac River. Their family now included two of Martha's grandchildren, George Washington Parke Custis and Eleanor (Nelly) Parke Custis, the two younger children of her son, Jackie.

Five years later, the new nation's constitution was ratified, and George Washington became America's first president in 1789. At the age of fifty-seven, Martha found herself occupying an unprecedented position: the wife of an American president. She was expected to establish the role of the nation's hostess and create a style that would bear no resemblance to British royalty yet would command dignity and respect. The new nation's citizens were in

ABOVE: *Martha Washington, or Lady Washington as she came to be known, was expected to invent the role of first lady. She handled the position with poise and dignity, though she preferred the quiet life of the Mount Vernon plantation.*

ABOVE: *This painting portrays George Washington sitting for his portrait by Gilbert Stuart. Among those looking on is Martha, who commissioned the famous work of art.*

OPPOSITE: *Martha Washington wore this salmon-colored dress more than two hundred years ago. The hand-painted silk features a trellis pattern with four different flower motifs and a variety of insects.*

a dilemma about what to call Martha and finally settled on "Lady Washington."

On Friday evenings in the house in which the president and first lady resided on Cherry Street in New York City, Martha held receptions, referred to as drawing rooms, which were open to the public—both men and women. At her first Friday evening drawing room, the guests were uncertain whether they should leave before their hostess or if they should wait for her to retire for the night. Sensing their concern, Martha announced, "The General always retires at nine and I generally precede him." She then left the room, thereby

freeing her guests from any worry of offending their hostess.

In addition to her Friday evening drawing rooms, Martha hosted dinners and receptions honoring government officials and foreign visitors. Her warm hospitality and unpretentious manner put guests at ease. Even though Martha could easily have afforded the most stylish European fashions, she generally opted for modest, homespun American-made dresses.

Being the nation's hostess did not involve only entertaining at home. Etiquette dictated that she visit all ladies who left their calling cards at the president's home. Sometimes this meant that the first lady had to stop by more than fifteen residences in one day. In a letter to her friend Mercy Otis Warren, dated December 26, 1789, she wrote, "I sometimes think the arrangement is not quite as it ought to have been, that I, who had much rather be at home, should occupy a place with which a great many younger and gayer women would be prodigiously pleased."

No doubt Mrs. Washington would have preferred to stay at home, but being the wife of America's first president came with such obligations as presiding over receptions, dinners, and ceremonial occasions. As a hostess, she never allowed her guests to talk about politics, steering them instead to noncontroversial topics. When the Cherry Street residence became too small to accommodate the large number of guests, the Washingtons moved to a larger house on Broadway. However, they had barely settled into the new home when the nation's capital moved to Philadelphia, a change that occurred in 1790.

With the end of President Washington's administration in 1797, he and Martha were finally able to retire to Mount Vernon, where they could relax with their family and friends. Martha was overjoyed to resume her life as the wife of a Virginia planter. Unfortunately, this happiness ended with the death of her beloved husband in December 1799. Martha survived President Washington by almost two and a half years. The couple are buried next to each other on their Mount Vernon estate.

ABIGAIL SMITH ADAMS

November 22, 1744–October 28, 1818

John Adams, president 1797–1801

"If man is Lord, woman is Lordess, that is what I contend for and if a woman does not hold the Reigns [sic] of Government, I see no reason for her not judging how they are conducted."

—Abigail Adams

OPPOSITE: *Gilbert Stuart began this portrait of Abigail Smith Adams in 1800— the same year in which she and President John Adams moved into the unfinished Executive Mansion. The couple were the first to live in the White House.*

Abigail Smith, the second of three sisters, was born in 1744 to the Reverend William Smith and Elizabeth Quincy in the coastal town of Weymouth, Massachusetts, near Boston. Abigail's forebears were Congregational ministers and prominent citizens in the colonies. Although she had no formal education, she was an enthusiastic reader with a sharp mind. By the time she was fifteen, she had mastered the works of Shakespeare.

Abigail regularly took part in intellectual conversations with her father's guests. One frequent visitor was John Adams, a lawyer nine years older than she. Adams was impressed by the young woman's wit and intellect. In 1764, five years after becoming acquainted, the two were married, embarking upon a partnership that lasted fifty-four years. They became the parents of five children (four of whom lived to maturity), including the future sixth president of the United States, John Quincy Adams.

Abigail and John Adams endured lengthy separations from each other while John was a representative to the Continental Congress and later a diplomat in Europe. During these absences, Abigail

RIGHT: *In this letter to her husband dated December 14, 1796, Abigail Adams discusses the upcoming presidential election.*

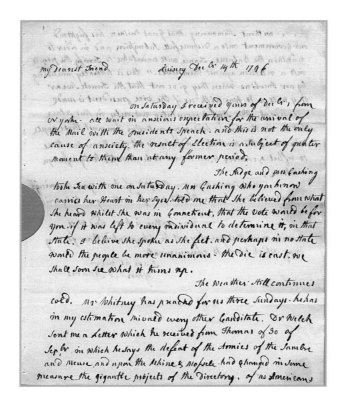

with other patriotic women prior to and during the American Revolution, she supported embargoes on British imports such as tea and fabrics.

Known for their prolific correspondence, John and Abigail sent hundreds of letters to each other, hers beginning with "My Dearest Friend." She was a staunch supporter of women's rights and equal educational opportunities for women. In one letter—dated March 31, 1776—to her husband when he was a representative to the Second Continental Congress, she wrote, "[I]n the new code of laws, which I suppose it will be necessary for you to make, I desire you would remember the ladies and be more generous and favorable to them than your ancestors."

In 1797, John Adams was sworn in as president of the United States. It was a tumultuous time for the newborn country, which was still defining itself. Abigail was delayed for two months in joining her newly elected husband in the temporary capital of Philadelphia. Missing her presence and political acumen, the new president wrote for her to hurry to join him, stating, "I never wanted your advice and assistance more in my life." Indeed, Mrs. Adams often expressed her opinions on policy and presented her views regarding his speeches. Their recognized partnership brought sarcastic comments from the chief executive's political enemies, who referred to Abigail as "Mrs. President."

When it came to acting as the nation's hostess, Abigail Adams boasted a lively entertainment style that differed dramatically from Martha Washington's simple and unpretentious manner. Whereas Martha never engaged in political dialogue, Abigail enjoyed spirited conversations and political debates. Her afternoons were often filled receiving guests and returning calls to the ladies who left their cards at the president's home.

In November 1800, President and Mrs. Adams moved from Philadelphia to the nation's new

became adept at not only raising and educating their children but also managing their farm in Braintree (now Quincy), Massachusetts. She supervised the planting and harvesting, bought stock, paid bills, and oversaw the dairy, all the while dealing with wartime inflation and shortages. Along

capital city of Washington, D.C., where they were the first presidential couple to inhabit what was then only informally known as the White House. At the time, the structure was called the President's House or the Executive Mansion. When the Adamses moved in, the building was still unfinished. Not only did they have to use a temporary staircase, but the plaster on the walls was still wet, resulting in the need to have fires burning constantly in thirteen fireplaces. An oppressive dampness permeated the mansion, making the residents quite uncomfortable. What's more, the furniture was unbefitting a presidential couple, as it was worn and tattered from use in previous presidential homes.

President and Mrs. Adams opened the Executive Mansion to the public on January 1, 1801, giving citizens their first glimpse inside. This New Year's Day tradition of welcoming the public into the president's home—a custom initiated by Mrs. Washington—would last more than one hundred years.

When John Adams failed in his attempt for reelection, he and Abigail retired to their home in Massachusetts. Abigail died at the age of seventy-three, only six years before her son John Quincy Adams was elected president. The diaries and letters left by Abigail Adams have given historians firsthand insight into domestic and political life during a turbulent time in America's history.

ABOVE: *This 1966 painting by Gordon Phillips shows Abigail Adams supervising the hanging of laundry in the unfinished East Room of the White House. Abigail felt that hanging the president's laundry outside would be undignified.*

DOLLEY PAYNE TODD MADISON

May 20, 1768–July 12, 1849
James Madison, president 1809–1817

"Our kind friend, Mr. Carroll, has come to hasten my departure, and is in a very bad humor with me because I insist on waiting until the large picture of Gen. Washington is secured….I have ordered the frame to be broken and the canvas taken out; it is done, and the precious portrait placed in the hands of two gentlemen of New York for safe keeping. And now, dear sister, I must leave this house."

—Dolley Madison in a letter to her sister Anna Cutts as British troops approached the capital city, August 23, 1814

Dolley Payne, the second of six children, was born on May 20, 1768, in Guilford County, North Carolina. Her parents, John and Mary Payne, raised her in the Quaker faith. A year after her birth, the family moved to Hanover County, Virginia, and then in 1783 relocated to Philadelphia, where John started a starch business. After that venture failed, Dolley's mother opened their home to boarders.

At the age of twenty-one, Dolley married John Todd, a lawyer who was also a Quaker. Only a few years later, in 1793, the yellow fever epidemic, which killed thousands of Philadelphia citizens, claimed the lives of her husband and the younger of their two sons. Widowed with a little boy to raise, Dolley went to work in her mother's boardinghouse. By this time Philadelphia had become the capital city, and Dolley got to know several congressmen who stayed at her mother's home.

It was through this circle that Dolley became acquainted with her second husband, James Madison. Known as "the Great Little Madison" because of his five-foot-four-inch (163cm) frame, James was a congressman from Virginia at the time. The two were introduced by a mutual friend, Aaron Burr, then a senator from New York. On September 15, 1794, the future president and Dolley were married. Their union resulted in Dolley's expulsion from the Quaker faith because James was an Episcopalian. However, the gregarious Mrs. Madison readily gave up her traditional gray Quaker garb for a more flamboyant wardrobe better suited to her personality.

When her husband became president in 1809, Dolley was more than prepared for the role of first lady; she had frequently served as hostess during the previous eight years for widowed president Thomas Jefferson, under whom her husband had served as secretary of state. For President Madison's inaugural ball—the first to be held in Washington, D.C., at Long's Hotel on Capitol Hill—she donned a beige velvet dress, which showed off her buxom figure and flattered her five-foot-eight-inch (173cm) height. Crowning the ensemble was a purple turban embellished with white satin and huge white plumes.

Dolley was a master at making all guests feel comfortable. A great asset to her husband, she often used this talent to calm antagonistic politicians. In fact, it was said that her easy manner made it difficult to know if she were speaking with a friend or a political enemy. She possessed a remarkable ability to remember names, and her outgoing demeanor contrasted with her reticent husband's disposition. At dinners, it was Dolley who presided

at the head of the table, with guests seated on her right and left. President Madison preferred to sit at a side table where he wouldn't be expected to engage in conversation.

Dolley made an impact not only on Washington society but on the Executive Mansion itself. Though carpeting had been replaced and some pieces reupholstered during Thomas Jefferson's presidency, many of the furnishings were worn and tattered from their use during previous administrations. When Congress appropriated $11,000 to buy new furnishings for the President's House, Dolley wasted no time removing the faded red draperies,

ABOVE: *Dolley Madison posed for this portrait by Gilbert Stuart in 1804. At the time, her husband, James Madison, was secretary of state, serving under President Thomas Jefferson. During the widowed Jefferson's two terms in office—from 1801 to 1809—Dolley stepped in as the nation's hostess. She then continued in the role of first lady for another eight years after her husband became chief executive in 1809.*

RIGHT: *William S. Elwell painted this portrait of an elderly Dolley Madison in February 1848—a little over a year before her death. In his diary, Elwell described the queen of Washington society as "a very estimable lady, kind and obliging, one of the Old School."*

replacing them with cheery yellow, and buying sofas and chairs to match. Within eight weeks, she was ready to show off the newly redecorated oval room (now known as the Blue Room) on the main floor during her first drawing room. Her regular Wednesday evening drawing rooms, which were open to anyone, were often so crowded that they became known as "Mrs. Madison's squeezes." In addition to hosting these weekly events, Dolley continued the practice of returning calls. Because Washington's unpaved streets made travel within the city difficult, this task took a great deal of time, often consuming entire days. Nonetheless, Mrs. Madison carried out the responsibility, as she knew that not doing so could result in the making of a new political enemy for her husband.

During the War of 1812, only moments before the British invaded the capital city, Dolley Madison stayed in the President's House to make sure that vital state papers, silver, household items, and Gilbert Stuart's portrait of George Washington were safely out of the building. In a letter to her sister Anna Cutts, dated August 23, 1814, she hurriedly wrote, "[O]ur private property must be sacrificed." After the British burned the President's House, James and Dolley Madison relocated to another Washington residence known as the Octagon House, where they stayed for the remainder of his term. There, Mrs. Madison continued as the social leader of Washington, happily showing off her customary vibrant-colored garments, trademark turbans, and feather plumes.

In 1817, at the end of James' second term, the Madisons retired to Montpelier, James' Virginia estate. Their forty-one-year marriage ended with his death in 1836. Sadly, Dolley's son, John Payne Todd, mismanaged the estate, leaving his mother destitute and essentially homeless. Dolley returned to Washington, where she was taken care of by her many friends and welcomed as the guest of honor at countless social and political events. She also continued to be an active presence in the Executive Mansion as a frequent visitor and unofficial advisor to subsequent first ladies.

As a perpetual force in Washington, Dolley continued to make her mark on history. In 1844, when Samuel Morse demonstrated the electric telegraph between Washington and Baltimore, Dolley was inside the Capitol building at the time that the famous first message, "What hath God wrought," was sent. Morse asked the elderly Mrs. Madison if she would like to transmit a message. Knowing that her friend was with the group at the other end of the line in Baltimore, Dolley sent the following statement: "Message from Mrs. Madison. She sends her love to Mrs. Wethered." Thus, Dolley Madison sent the first personal correspondence ever delivered by telegraph.

The much admired queen of Washington society died peacefully on July 12, 1849, at the age of eighty-one. She is buried next to her husband in the family cemetery at Montpelier.

LEFT: *This intricately embroidered open robe worn by Dolley Madison features a high waist and a diamond-shaped back that shows off the train.*

ELIZABETH KORTRIGHT MONROE

June 30, 1768–September 23, 1830
James Monroe, president 1817–1825

"The dinner was served in the French style….Of attendants there were a good many. They were neatly dressed, out of livery, and sufficient….the whole entertainment might have passed for a better sort of European dinner party at which the guests were too numerous for general or very agreeable discourse and some of them too new to be entirely at ease."

—James Fenimore Cooper commenting on a White House dinner in 1824

n February 1795, when her husband, James Monroe, was ambassador to France, Elizabeth Kortright Monroe learned that the wife and children of America's Revolutionary ally the Marquis de Lafayette were being held prisoner, soon to be executed. Mrs. Monroe boarded a coach and drove through the streets of Paris to the prison, where she announced flamboyantly that she was there to visit the marquise. Desiring to stay on good terms with the United States, the French officials released the Marquise de Lafayette and her children. Elizabeth Monroe was credited with saving their lives and became known as La Belle Américaine.

Born in New York City in June 1768, Elizabeth Kortright was one of five children of Hannah Aspinwall and Captain Lawrence Kortright, the latter a wealthy New York merchant. Elizabeth and her siblings enjoyed all the privileges of being born into affluence and New York society. Tutored at home, they enjoyed an education that was not common for their time. Part of their education included French lessons, which Elizabeth found much use for on jaunts to Europe with her sisters and later—and more importantly—when her husband held diplomatic posts in London and Paris.

Elizabeth met James Monroe in 1785 while he was serving as a representative from Virginia to the Continental Congress. The two were married at New York's fashionable Trinity Church on February 16, 1786, and ultimately became the parents of one son (who lived only two years) and two daughters. In 1816, after serving as a senator, diplomat, governor, and cabinet member, James Monroe was elected president. James and Elizabeth spent the first seven months of his administration at the Octagon House, where the Madisons had lived after the President's House was nearly destroyed by fire during the War of 1812. In October 1817, the Monroes—along with their daughter Eliza; her husband, George Hay; and the Hays' daughter—moved into the rebuilt Executive Mansion.

Congress appropriated $20,000 to outfit the White House. However, the Monroes felt that this sum was inadequate. Congress later acquiesced and agreed to increase the funds to a total of $50,000. In addition to ordering furniture, the Monroes purchased a $1,200 silver centerpiece—more than fourteen feet (4.3m) long and two feet (61cm) wide—boasting bronze garlands of fruit and crystal vases and candleholders. This piece (gilded during the Van Buren administration) is still in use at the White House today.

The New Year's Day open house in 1818 gave the public its first glimpse of the restored and redecorated mansion. The atmosphere was strikingly different from the tone that had been set by the previous first lady. Not only was Dolley Madison's former comfortable and sunny home now cold and formal, adorned with gilded wood and silk furniture, but the new first lady's wardrobe was unmistakably French and very expensive. Heightening the rigid atmosphere, Mrs. Monroe sat on a raised platform to receive guests while uniformed guards stood at the door turning away inappropriately dressed citizens.

ABOVE: *A petite beauty, Elizabeth Monroe was approximately five feet (150cm) tall and weighed about ninety pounds (40.8kg). Her wardrobe and lifestyle were greatly influenced by the French, and her manner was considered regal and aloof.*

ABOVE: *This circa 1817 centerpiece was purchased for the White House by President and Mrs. Monroe. Fruits and vines, as well as figures of Bacchus and bacchantes, are featured in the elaborate design.*

As first lady, Mrs. Monroe was considered aloof and regal. Pleading ill health, she often had one of her daughters fill in for her as hostess at White House functions. Citing the same excuse, she also frequently ignored the responsibility of paying return visits when ladies left their calling cards at the White House. This blatant violation of protocol left Washington society seething. Adding fuel to the fire was the wedding of the Monroes' younger daughter,

Maria, which was arranged as a private family affair rather than being the large society event expected by Washington's leading families. Washingtonians retaliated by refusing invitations to the White House when they knew that one of the Monroe daughters would be acting as the stand-in hostess.

Undeniably, Elizabeth Kortright Monroe irritated Washington society by making no secret of the fact that she considered herself an aristocrat.

ABOVE: *President and Mrs. Monroe commissioned Pierre-Louis Dagoty and Edouard Honoré of Paris to design a dessert service (circa 1817) for the White House. The china pattern features a patriotic motif with a stylized eagle in the center and five vignettes depicting science, art, commerce, agriculture, and strength on the maroon border.*

However, it is important to note that this independent woman refused to compromise her identity in order to promote her husband's political agenda and please others. Her refusal to return visits—a laborious occupation—and her willingness to decorate, entertain, and dress in a manner of her own choosing paved the way for future first ladies to bring their own distinct personalities and styles to the role of the nation's hostess.

After leaving the White House in 1825, the Monroes retired to Oak Hill, their estate in Virginia. Elizabeth died on September 23, 1830; her husband died less than a year later. (He was the third of five presidents to die on the Fourth of July.) The couple are buried next to each other in Hollywood Cemetery in Richmond, Virginia.

LOUISA CATHERINE JOHNSON ADAMS

February 12, 1775–May 14, 1852
John Quincy Adams, president 1825–1829

*"I cannot believe there is any inferiority in the sexes, as far as the mind and intellect
are concerned, and man is aware of the fact."*

—Louisa Adams

OPPOSITE: *This portrait
(circa 1794) of a young Louisa
Adams was painted by
American artist Edward
Savage. The daughter of an
American merchant, Louisa
was born in England and
educated in both England
and France. Her in-laws, John
and Abigail Adams, did not
appreciate her European
manners.*

Louisa Catherine Johnson—daughter of
Catherine Nuth, a British citizen, and Joshua
Johnson, an American businessman—entered the
world in 1775 in London, making her the only
first lady born outside the United States. It was
in London that she met John Quincy Adams, then
a diplomat from America. When the two were
married on July 26, 1797, John—according to the
presiding minister—said to his bride that he loved
her "but I love my country more." As one might
suspect from this statement, the couple's marriage
was strained from the beginning. John expected
Louisa to follow his every command and made

decisions about their lives without consulting her.
During their marriage, Louisa was pregnant eleven
times; three sons lived to maturity.

In 1809, President Madison appointed John
Quincy Adams as America's first minister to
Russia. During the autumn of that year, John and
Louisa left for Saint Petersburg, taking Charles,
their youngest son, with them. Their two other
children, John and George, stayed behind in
Massachusetts with their grandparents. In 1814,
Adams was sent to Belgium to negotiate the Treaty
of Ghent, which officially ended the War of 1812.
Once that mission had been accomplished, he sent

RIGHT: *This white silk dress, which was worn by Louisa Adams, is enhanced by netting and metallic thread around the neckline, sleeves, waist, and base of the skirt.*

word to Louisa in Saint Petersburg to dispose of their property and join him in Paris. The dutiful wife made the thousand-mile journey with Charles across Russia, enduring the hardships of a Russian winter and the military challenges of the Napoleonic War. Her bravery in the face of life-threatening danger impressed even her reserved husband.

In 1817, John Quincy Adams became secretary of state under President Monroe, but John's ultimate goal was the presidency. Believing that his many years of public service entitled him to the position, he refused to actively run for office. However, he instructed Louisa to campaign for him, which she did by visiting other cities and entertaining congressmen, senators, and their wives. In the mornings, he would make a list of people she was to call on, often as many as twenty-five per day. Ultimately, these efforts were successful, as John Quincy Adams was elected America's sixth president in 1824.

By the time she entered the White House, Louisa was already an accomplished hostess. Even though her European manner was considered to be generally stiff and formal, her weekly drawing rooms—always open to the public—were more relaxed. Unlike her predecessor, Elizabeth Monroe, Louisa chose to undertake the exhausting task of visiting women who left their calling cards at the White House. Although she detested the ritual, she understood its importance to her husband's career. She once wrote in her diary, "Oh these visits have made me sick many times and I really sometimes think they will make me crazy."

With the exception of the weekly drawing rooms, entertaining was kept to a minimum. Although Louisa was a talented musician who excelled at playing the harp and spinet, she rarely played because her husband felt that engaging in such pursuits was beneath the dignity of the first lady. Her strained and sometimes antagonistic marriage led her to find other outlets for self-fulfillment, such as cultivating silkworms, reading, and translating French literature. In her unpublished diary, which she titled "Adventures of a Nobody," she wrote in detail about her marriage to a reserved, cold, and inconsiderate husband who had little respect for women.

Although John Quincy Adams was defeated for reelection in 1828, he was not ready to give up politics. In 1830, he was elected to the House of Representatives, where he served for seventeen years—until the time of his death. The couple settled into a more tranquil life during this period, and even though their marriage was still strained, Louisa noted in her diary that it was the best period of their lives. On February 21, 1848, during a debate in Congress, John suffered a stroke. He died on February 23. When Louisa Adams died four years later at the age of seventy-seven, Congress adjourned to attend her funeral.

LEFT: *Louisa was an accomplished musician who played the spinet and harp. Her love for the latter is represented in this circa 1824 portrait by American artist Charles Bird King (who studied under Edward Savage). A woman of many talents, Louisa was fluent in French and Greek and enjoyed translating classic literature into English.*

ANGELICA SINGLETON VAN BUREN

February 13, 1816–December 29, 1877
Martin Van Buren, president 1837–1841

"Angelica Van Buren is a lady of rare accomplishments, very modest yet perfectly easy and graceful in her manners and free and vivacious in her conversation. She is universally admired."

—Boston Post *reporting on the 1839 New Year's Day White House open house*

When Martin Van Buren became America's eighth president in 1837, he had been a widower for eighteen years. In 1819, Hannah Hoes Van Buren had died, leaving her husband four sons ranging in age from two to twelve.

When he entered the White House with his grown sons, Van Buren, who had been accustomed to refined living, was dismayed by the deteriorated condition of the furnishings that had not been updated since the Monroes had lived there a dozen years earlier. The pieces that were not up to par were replaced at a cost of $25,000. Because of the color of the new upholstery in the first-floor oval drawing room, that space became known as the Blue Room. The Van Burens actually lived more comfortably than any previous first family, as the house was equipped with running water—which had been connected during Andrew Jackson's administration (1829–1837)—and an updated heating system. Even though the White House had been in desperate need of refurbishing, the president ended up receiving much criticism for spending money to remedy the problem during a severe economic depression.

LEFT: *This portrait features Angelica Singleton Van Buren at the age of twenty-six, four years after her marriage to Abraham Van Buren. Painted by Henry Inman in 1842, the work of art is prominently displayed above a fireplace in the Red Room at the White House. Jackie Kennedy stated that this portrait was her favorite of all those in the White House collection depicting first ladies.*

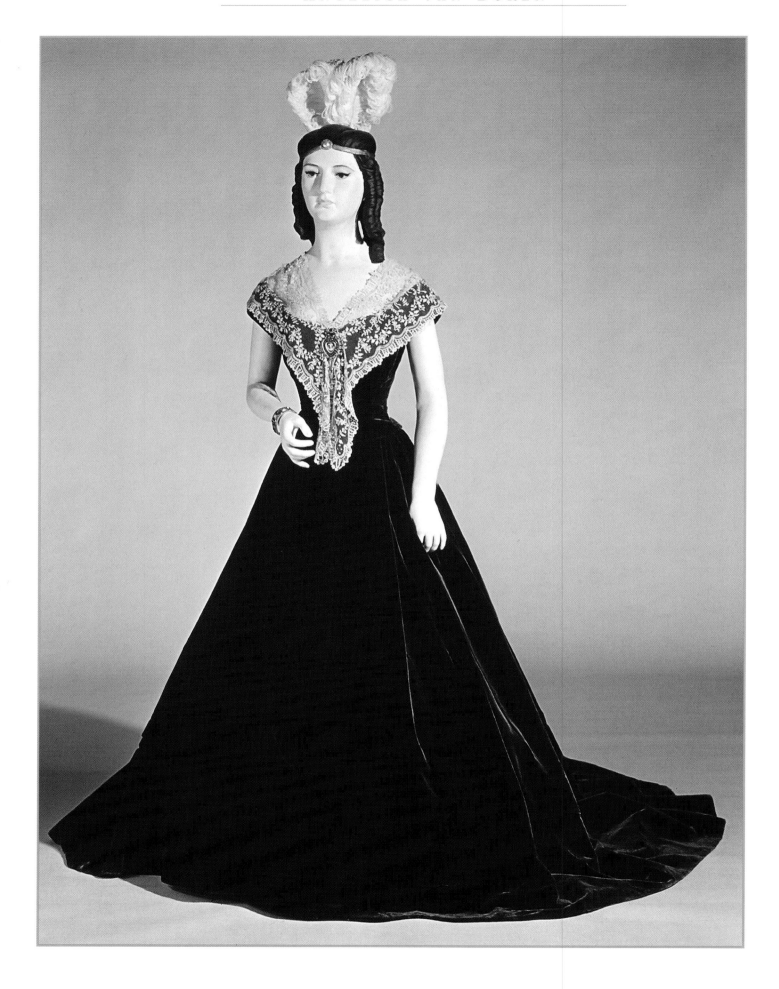

The widowed president depended on female friends or the wives of members of the Senate and House to preside at dinners as his official White House hostess. One woman who often assisted him in this regard was former first lady Dolley Madison. When Dolley decided that the White House needed a more permanent female fixture, she introduced Angelica Singleton, her beautiful twenty-two-year-old cousin from South Carolina, to the president and his sons.

Abraham Van Buren, the eldest son, was smitten by the raven-haired beauty, and on November 27, 1838, at the home of Angelica's family, the pair became husband and wife. Their honeymoon trip to Europe, which took place the following spring, included a visit with Angelica's cousin Andrew Stevenson, who was minister to Great Britain. He introduced his guests to royalty and arranged for Angelica to receive the honor of being presented to Queen Victoria. In Paris, the newlyweds were presented to the king and queen of France, who gave them a private tour of the palace.

When the couple returned to Washington, Abraham resumed his duties as his father's private secretary. At the president's request, Angelica became the official White House hostess. Not sure what was expected of her as first lady, Angelica decided to use the royal courts that she had seen in Europe as her model. At her first reception, she received guests from an improvised throne, wearing a purple velvet dress with a long train, ostrich plumes in her hair, and pearls. For hours she sat on her throne, smiling, remaining silent, and looking regal.

Angelica's polished style complemented the president's own refined manners and elegant taste. The rowdy crowds that had descended on the White House during Andrew Jackson's administration were no longer welcome. Van Buren even went so far as to place a guard at the door to turn away anyone who seemed improper. In strong contrast to

the tone set by the previous president, a powerful sense of decorum pervaded White House events. While Van Buren enjoyed small elegant dinners with friends, he banned nearly all public receptions except the traditional New Year's Day open house, at which he didn't serve food or drinks.

After leaving the White House, Angelica and her husband lived in South Carolina and Europe, eventually making their home in New York City. Her portrait is prominently displayed in the Red Room of the White House, where it has become a favorite of White House families and visitors.

OPPOSITE: *This gown was worn by the elegant Angelica Singleton Van Buren, who brought a regal sense of style to the White House.*

ABOVE: *Hannah Hoes Van Buren, wife of Martin Van Buren, was born in Kinderhook, New York, in 1783. She died of tuberculosis on February 5, 1819.*

ANNA TUTHILL SYMMES HARRISON

July 25, 1775–February 25, 1864

William Henry Harrison, president 1841

"I wish that my husband's friends had left him where he is,

happy and contented in retirement."

—Anna Harrison upon learning that her husband had been elected president

Anna Tuthill Symmes, the second child of New Jersey Supreme Court judge John Cleves Symmes and Anna Tuthill, was born in Morristown, New Jersey, on July 25, 1775. When Anna was three years old, her mother died, at which point she and her older sister were sent to stay with their wealthy maternal grandparents on Long Island, where she lived until she was seventeen. Anna attended many schools, including Clinton Academy and Miss Graham's Boarding School in New York City. When she was nineteen, she joined her father and his second wife at their home in North Bend, Ohio, near the Cincinnati River.

Twenty-two-year-old army captain William Henry Harrison was quite taken with the sophisticated, charming, and well-educated Anna Symmes, two and a half years his junior, when he became acquainted with her. It was not long before he proposed marriage. But Anna's father, knowing the hardships that his daughter would face traveling from post to post as the wife of a career soldier, refused to give the couple his consent. This lack of a blessing, however, did not stop the young sweethearts; when Anna's father left town on a business trip, she and William eloped, exchanging vows on November 25, 1795. The couple eventually had ten children, nine of whom lived to adulthood. Anna took over the responsibility of educating their children. She also developed a reputation for being a welcoming hostess to itinerant preachers, other travelers, and relatives.

William resigned his commission in 1798, when President John Adams appointed him secretary of the Northwest Territory. Two years later, in 1800, he was appointed territorial governor of Indiana. During the War of 1812, William was commissioned a major general, later rising to brigadier general in command of the Northwest frontier. His leadership in the Battle of the Thames secured the Northwest, making him a national hero. He went on to serve as a U.S. congressman, an Ohio state senator, and a U.S. senator before being elected America's ninth president in 1840. Anna was disappointed that her husband had been elected, preferring that he stay home and tend their farm.

Sixty-five years old when her husband was elected, Anna was too ill to accompany her husband on the arduous winter journey from North Bend to Washington, D.C. In her stead, the president-elect took several relatives with him, including his son's widow, Jane Irwin Harrison, whom he asked to perform the duties of White House hostess until Anna was able to make it to the capital city that spring.

On March 4, 1841, William Henry Harrison delivered an inaugural address that lasted one hour and forty minutes—in the midst of wind and rain. Afterward, the new president developed a cold that turned into pneumonia. Only one month later, on April 4, the president died. He was temporarily buried in Washington, and in June of that year, his remains were moved to the family cemetery in North Bend.

While Anna was preparing to join her husband, she learned of his death. Congress awarded her her husband's entire first-year salary of $25,000. She continued to reside at their home in North Bend until a fire destroyed it in the 1850s. She then moved in with her son Congressman John Scott Harrison, who owned a vast estate in North Bend. John Scott Harrison was the father of Benjamin Harrison, who would become America's twenty-third president.

Anna survived her husband by almost twenty-three years. She died in February of 1864 at the age of eighty-eight and is buried next to her husband in North Bend.

ABOVE: *Anna Symmes Harrison was one of the thousands of women who traveled westward during the early years of our nation. Along with other pioneer women, Anna endured the isolation and primitive conditions of frontier life.*

LETITIA CHRISTIAN TYLER

November 12, 1790–September 10, 1842
John Tyler, president 1841–1845

"The suite of rooms on the ground floor were lighted up and a military band was playing in the hall. In the smaller drawing room, the center of a circle of company were the President and his daughter-in-law, who acted as lady of the mansion, and a very interesting, graceful and accomplished lady too."

—*Charles Dickens commenting on a reception held for himself and Washington Irving in March 1842*

OPPOSITE: *Letitia Tyler was confined to her room during her husband's tenure as president. Born on November 12, 1790, she was the first wife of a president to enter the world as an American citizen.*

Letitia Christian was born in New Kent County, Virginia, near Williamsburg. She met John Tyler at a party and, after a five-year courtship, married him on March 29, 1813, at Cedar Grove, her family's estate. The couple became the parents of five daughters and three sons; their daughter Anne died at birth.

Preferring domestic life to participating in her husband's political career, Letitia spent her time taking care of matters at home. At the age of forty-nine, she suffered a stroke, which left her partially paralyzed. In 1841, when John Tyler became William Henry Harrison's vice president, Tyler planned to fulfill his duties in Williamsburg, where his wife was confined to an invalid's chair. But only a month after Tyler took the oath of vice president, newly elected President William Harrison contracted pneumonia and died. Tyler succeeded him as president and moved his family to Washington.

During her time in the White House, Letitia remained out of the public eye, keeping to the second-floor family quarters where her second daughter, also named Letitia, stayed to take care of her. In the first lady's absence, the Tylers' daughter-in-law Priscilla Cooper Tyler filled in as official White House hostess. Advising her in this capacity was former first lady Dolley Madison. Priscilla had been a professional actress who had traveled around the country performing in plays with her father, actor Thomas Cooper. Accustomed to being in the limelight, she relished her role as hostess. She once wrote in her diary, "I am considered 'charmante' by the Frenchmen, 'lovely' by the Americans and 'really quite nice, you know' by the English."

With the help of Priscilla, President Tyler entertained often. They hosted a drawing room every evening and a private ball for friends and statesmen during the winter. In the summer, they hosted a Marine Band concert on the White House lawn and a Fourth of July open house, in addition to continuing the traditional New Year's Day open house. One of the largest receptions that they threw was in honor of Charles Dickens and Washington Irving—an event at which three thousand people crowded into the Great Audience Room, also known as the East Room, hoping to get a glimpse of the literary celebrities.

The only public appearance that Letitia made as first lady was on January 31, 1842, at the wedding of her daughter Elizabeth, held in the East Room. Among the guests were statesmen, friends, and, of course, the reigning queen of Washington society, Dolley Madison. Less than a year later, on September 10, 1842, Letitia Christian Tyler died, making her the first of the nation's first ladies to die during her husband's administration. After a state funeral held in the White House, she was buried at Cedar Grove.

JULIA GARDINER TYLER

May 4, 1820–July 10, 1889
John Tyler, president 1841–1845

"I have commenced my auspicious reign and am in quiet possession

of the Presidential mansion."

—Julia Tyler in a letter to her mother, 1844

After the death of Letitia Tyler, much of the entertaining at the White House was suspended, with the exception of quiet evenings with close friends. Among these privileged guests were Julia Gardiner—a socialite from New York—and her parents. It wasn't long before the president took a romantic interest in the young woman.

Julia was born into wealth at her family's estate on Gardiners Island, New York, in 1820. Tutored at home until she was sixteen, she was then sent to a finishing school in New York, after which she set off on an extensive trip to Europe. Known as "the Rose of Long Island," the dark-haired beauty once

shocked and embarrassed her parents by posing for a department store advertisement.

In February 1844, while on a visit to Washington, Julia and her father were invited aboard the military steamer *Princeton*, along with other dignitaries including the ever-present Dolley Madison. During a demonstration of a large cannon, the weapon exploded, killing several people onboard, among them the secretary of the navy, the secretary of state, and Julia's father. After this tragedy, the president and Julia became closer. When John Tyler asked Mrs. Gardiner for permission to marry her daughter, she replied that she

LEFT: *As a debutante, Julia Gardiner started a fashion craze by wearing a diamond, held in place with a gold chain, on her forehead. Julia donated this portrait, painted in 1848 by Francesco Anelli, to the White House.*

BELOW: *This 1839 advertisement for Bogert and Mecamly's department store features a young Julia Gardiner. Her appearance in the advertisement was a source of embarrassment for her family, as it was not considered proper for a woman of her social standing.*

"would acquiesce only if he could provide necessary comforts and elegancies of life."

John Tyler and Julia Gardiner were married at the Church of the Ascension in New York City on June 26, 1844, making Tyler the first president to marry while in office. He was fifty-four at the time. His bride was thirty years younger than he—and five years younger than his eldest daughter.

Julia delighted in her position as first lady. With her family money, she purchased new French furniture for the White House, bought a new wardrobe for herself, and stocked the pantry with French wine. She told her mother, "I intend to do something in the way of entertaining that shall be the admiration and talk of the Washington world." And she did. At her first drawing room, she wore a headdress bearing enough jewels to make it look like a crown and she received guests while seated in a large armchair on a raised platform surrounded by twelve maids of honor all wearing white.

On the political front, Julia regularly attended Congress and heartily supported Tyler's campaign for the annexation of Texas. After the president signed the bill, which Julia referred to as "my annexation bill," she proudly wore the pen he had used on a gold chain around her neck.

After Tyler's term in the White House was over, he and Julia retired to his Virginia estate, Sherwood Forest, where over time Julia gave birth to five sons and two daughters. Their last child was born in 1860, when John Tyler was seventy years old. The former president died less than two years later. Upon the defeat of the Confederacy, Julia was left practically penniless. In 1881, Congress voted to give her a $5,000 annual pension, which enabled her to live comfortably for the rest of her life. She is buried next to her husband in Richmond's Hollywood Cemetery.

BOGERT & MECAMLY
86

I'll Purchase at Bogert & Mecamly's No 86 9th Avenue. Their Goods Are Beautiful & Astonishingly Cheap

Lith & Pub. by Baker 8 Wall St. N.Y.

THE .... OF "Long Island."

LEFT: *Julia Tyler wore this gown of white mull during her brief time as first lady. Both skirt and bodice are embroidered with silver thread and a floral motif.*

SARAH CHILDRESS POLK

September 4, 1803–August 14, 1891
James K. Polk, president 1845–1849

"To dance in these rooms would be undignified and it would be respectful neither to the house nor to the office. How indecorous it would seem for dancing to be going on in one apartment while in another we were conversing with dignitaries of the republic or ministers of the gospel. This unseemly juxtaposition would be likely to occur at any time, were such amusements permitted."

—Sarah Polk

Sarah Childress grew up on a plantation near Murfreesboro, Tennessee. Her father was a wealthy planter and merchant who insisted that his children obtain a good education. Originally tutored at home, Sarah was later sent away to school in Nashville, Tennessee, and then to the Moravian Female Academy in Salem, North Carolina. As a result of her extensive schooling, Sarah was extremely well educated for a girl born in the early nineteenth century. She liked to read—newspapers especially—and enjoyed listening to political conversations between her father and his friend General Andrew Jackson.

Sarah met James Polk in 1821, when he was serving as chief clerk for the Tennessee House of Representatives. When he proposed, she said she would accept on one condition: that he run for a seat on the Tennessee state legislature. Polk did so and won, and the couple exchanged wedding vows on January 1, 1824.

Sarah delighted in her husband's political victories. From 1825 to 1839, James served as a member of Congress. When he decided to run for governor of Tennessee, Sarah became his unofficial campaign manager. She mailed literature, managed his schedule, and answered his correspondence. The campaign was successful, and in 1839, Polk became governor. While Sarah enjoyed her role as governor's wife, her ultimate goal was to be first lady of the nation.

Polk made his run for the White House in 1844. During the race for office, a supporter of Henry Clay, Polk's opponent, made the comment that Mrs. Clay would be a better first lady because she was an economical housekeeper and made excellent butter. Mrs. Polk responded that if she became first lady, she would be able to manage on her husband's $25,000 annual salary and wouldn't need to keep house or churn butter. In 1845, when she was forty-two, Sarah's dream was realized as her husband became the eleventh president of the United States.

On March 4, 1845, Sarah was oblivious to the driving rain as she proudly listened to her husband give his inaugural address. That evening, Sarah and James attended two inaugural balls. When the new president and first lady entered the celebrations, they insisted that all music and dancing be discontinued until they left. A staunch Presbyterian, Sarah banned card playing, hard liquor, and dancing in the White House. Additionally, she and her husband refused to work or receive visitors on Sunday. If unsuspecting guests made the mistake of calling upon the president on Sunday morning, Sarah deftly diffused the awkward situation by inviting them to church. When people complained about

her policies, President Polk replied that all domestic decisions fell within her area.

Sarah took her role as the president's advisor seriously. She edited his speeches, took care of his correspondence, and scanned newspapers for articles she thought might be of interest to him, marking them and leaving them on his desk. She also regularly attended sessions in the House of Representatives. Deeply interested in politics, she often became so engrossed with the topics of conversation at dinners with statesmen that she would forget about her meal. After dinners, the first lady

ABOVE: *Sarah Polk had the ability to charm even her husband's political enemies. On one occasion, she was overheard saying to Senator Henry Clay that if he defeated her husband she would happily surrender the White House to him. Senator Charles Sumner of Massachusetts once remarked after dining at the White House that Mrs. Polk's sweetness had won him over entirely.*

ignored her female guests, preferring instead to accompany the gentlemen to the parlor and continue what she considered more worthwhile and intriguing discussions. She championed her husband's cause of Manifest Destiny, believing that the United States was divinely driven to rule from sea to sea. In fact, she had such a great degree of influence with her husband that during the War with Mexico, President Polk rarely convened his cabinet, relying instead on the advice of his wife. During this time he wrote in his diary, "I have conducted the government without their aid....none but Sarah knew so intimately my private affairs."

Inarguably, Sarah preferred discussing affairs of state to hosting parties, but she well understood that entertaining was a necessary part of her role as first lady. Thus, she held drawing rooms on Tuesday and Friday evenings, though she offered no refreshments or entertainment. Often, she received visitors while she stood next to or behind her husband, along with her friend and ally Dolley Madison.

Although Sarah considered herself an equal in every way with her husband, she took little or no interest in women's rights until many years after she left the White House. When she learned that women were starting to go into the workforce she said, "It is now considered proper for young ladies, when they leave school, to teach or do something else for themselves. It was not so in my young days."

Sarah survived her husband by more than forty years. After his death in 1849, which occurred only months after he left office, she continued to reside at Polk Place, their home in Nashville, where she was honored as a distinguished citizen. During the Civil War, her home was declared neutral ground, and she received officers from both the North and the South. She stated, "I have always belonged, and do now belong to the whole country." Sarah Polk died just shy of her eighty-eighth birthday. She and her husband are entombed in Nashville.

LEFT: *Sarah Polk wore this blue brocade satin gown to the inaugural ball in 1845. The fan, which she carried that evening, was ordered by her husband for the occasion.*

BELOW: ***During Sarah Polk's time in the White House, forty-two rosewood chairs were commissioned for the State Dining Room. Upholstered in purple velvet, the balloon-backed chairs were made by cabinetmaker Charles A. Baudouine.***

MARGARET MACKALL SMITH TAYLOR

September 21, 1788–August 18, 1852
Zachary Taylor, president 1849–1850

"[Mrs. Taylor], full of interest in the passing show in which she had not the strength to take her part, talked most agreeably and kindly to the many friends who were admitted to her presence."

—Varina Howell Davis commenting on her several visits to Margaret Taylor

argaret "Peggy" Smith, born in Calvert County, Maryland, was the daughter of Ann Mackall and Walter Smith, the latter a prosperous planter who served in the Continental army as a major during the Revolutionary War. Margaret's education, which focused on needlework, music, and basic grammar, was typical for a girl born on a plantation in the eighteenth century. In 1809, while visiting a sister in Kentucky, she met young lieutenant Zachary Taylor. The two were married the following June. As the wife of a career military officer, Margaret followed her husband from one fort to another, living in log cabins, army barracks, or tents in the wilds of America's frontier. She gave birth to six children; three daughters and one son lived to maturity.

Knowing full well the hardships of life for a military wife, Margaret and Zachary were distressed when their second daughter, Sarah Knox Taylor, affectionately known as "Knoxy," announced her engagement to Lieutenant Jefferson Davis. They pleaded with their daughter to reconsider, but in 1835, Sarah married Davis without her parents' consent. Unfortunately, the newlyweds contracted malaria on their honeymoon, and Sarah died only three months later. Angry and bitter over the death of their beloved daughter, the Taylors blamed Davis; it would be ten years before they reconciled with him. When Davis remarried in 1845, his second wife, Varina, and Margaret Taylor became good friends.

When Zachary Taylor campaigned for the presidency in 1848, the opposition was reluctant to say anything negative about him, as he had been a hero of the Mexican War. Instead they attacked his wife. Margaret was portrayed as an uncouth, illiterate, vulgar woman who smoked a corncob pipe. None of these claims was accurate. In truth, Margaret Taylor was a pleasant, genteel lady with refined manners who couldn't tolerate pipe smoke because it made her ill. Despite the verbal attacks on his wife, on March 5, 1849, Zachary Taylor was sworn in as America's twelfth president. Margaret, then sixty years old, dreaded the idea of moving to Washington. She had become frail and chronically ill. Knowing she would be unable to perform the demanding duties required of her as first lady, Margaret depended on her youngest daughter, twenty-five-year-old Betty Bliss, to act as the nation's hostess.

On the evening of March 5, 1849, thousands of people celebrated at three inaugural balls in the capital city. Zachary Taylor attended each one accompanied by his daughter Betty. Mrs. Bliss, or "Miss Betty" as she was known, entertained often. She cheerfully held a weekly drawing room, hosted tea parties, and presided at receptions and dinners. Her father was also an amiable host, gladly shaking hands with anyone who introduced himself. As for Margaret, she rarely left the White House except to attend church services at St. John's Episcopal Church, which was only a short walk

LEFT: *Betty Taylor Bliss (pictured here) took over the duties of first lady on behalf of her chronically ill mother, Margaret Taylor. During the War with Mexico, Betty's husband, William W.S. Bliss, had served under her father (then a general) as chief of staff. When Taylor entered the White House, William became his private secretary.*

from the White House. She preferred staying upstairs in her brightly lit sitting room, where she would privately receive visitors and spend cherished time with her family. One friend whose company she particularly enjoyed was the wife of her former son-in-law, Mrs. Jefferson Davis, who when her daughter was unavailable stepped in as hostess of the White House.

Zachary Taylor's presidency abruptly came to an end in 1850. On July 4 of that year, he attended the Independence Day celebration at the Washington Monument. After sitting outside in the oppressive heat and humidity, he returned to the White House, where he ate cherries and drank a pitcher of milk. Later that day, he developed a gastrointestinal upset, common in Washington where poor sanitation made consuming raw fruit or milk dangerous. Five days later the president died, having served only sixteen months in office. Margaret Taylor survived her husband by two years. The couple are buried next to each other in Louisville, Kentucky.

ABIGAIL POWERS FILLMORE

March 13, 1798–March 30, 1853
Millard Fillmore, president 1850–1853

*"I have been much pleased with what I have seen of the president and his family,
and have been most kindly received by them."*

—*Washington Irving reflecting on a visit to the Fillmore White House*

Abigail Powers, born in Saratoga County, New York, near Albany, was the daughter of Abigail Newland and Lemuel Powers, the latter a Baptist minister. A year after his daughter's birth, the Reverend Powers died, leaving the family in financial distress. Abigail's mother decided to move the family to Cayuga County, still an undeveloped area in the western part of the state, with the hope that they could better subsist on their limited resources there. Tutored by her mother, Abigail was given an education that far exceeded what was typical for people living in the frontier. At the age of sixteen, Abigail herself became a teacher.

During the winter of 1819, Millard Fillmore walked into Abigail's classroom and declared himself a student. He had grown up in poverty on his family's farm and had received only a rudimentary education. When he was fourteen, his father had made him serve as an apprentice to a weaver, but Millard was determined to get an education and make a different path for himself.

Abigail and Millard's mutual love of books brought them together. After a lengthy courtship, they were married on February 5, 1826. The couple settled in East Aurora, New York, a town near Buffalo, where Millard practiced law. After the

birth of their second child, Abigail stopped teaching, but her love for learning never subsided. She went on to study French and taught herself to play the piano.

In the late 1820s, Millard began to focus on a political career. He started out as a representative for Erie County in the state assembly, became a member of Congress, and went on to serve as state comptroller for New York, after which he became Zachary Taylor's vice president. Abigail enjoyed living in Washington and being the wife of a statesman. She kept abreast of political issues, discussing them with her husband and friends. In July 1850, upon the death of President Taylor, Millard Fillmore became America's thirteenth president.

After the period of official mourning for Taylor ended, the Fillmores entertained frequently. They hosted a Tuesday morning drawing room and, when Congress was in session, a reception on

Fridays. In addition, they hosted a large dinner on Thursdays and a smaller one on Saturdays. There was no tobacco or alcohol at these events, as Fillmore had banned them, along with gambling, from the Executive Mansion. As often as possible, Abigail presided over these social functions. However, the effects of a severe ankle injury she had suffered earlier in life, along with her failing health, made standing or playing hostess to countless visitors difficult and sometimes painful. Often, she relied on her eighteen-year-old daughter, Mary Abigail (known as "Abby"), to take care of many of her social obligations. Neither the first lady nor her daughter returned social calls.

Abigail, whose love of reading began when she was a child, was appalled at the lack of books in the White House. After she petitioned Congress, $2,000 was appropriated for the purchase of books. Abigail happily chose numerous old and new

ABOVE: *As daguerreotypes became more readily available, the public became increasingly aware of what their first ladies looked like. The daguerreotype after which this image of Abigail Fillmore was created was a big seller, especially among women.*

such notables as William Thackeray, Washington Irving, and Charles Dickens.

President Fillmore often discussed political issues with his wife, and although he did not always agree with what she said, he listened to her opinions. It was well known that he would not take an important step without her counsel. While he went along with her advice on some matters, such as banning flogging from the navy, there were certain battles that Abigail lost; for instance, she was unable to keep him from signing the Fugitive Slave Bill, which allowed slave owners to reclaim their slaves even in free territory.

In 1852, Millard Fillmore was defeated in his bid for reelection by Franklin Pierce. During the outdoor inaugural ceremonies for the new president the following March, Abigail Fillmore stood in the snow and chilling wind next to her husband. Already in weak health, she developed pneumonia and died only a few weeks later. The House of Representatives and the Senate adjourned, and public offices shut down to honor her memory.

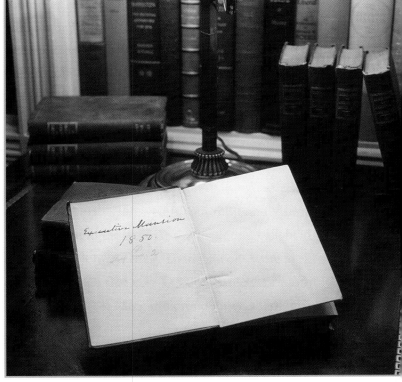

volumes as she transformed the upstairs oval sitting room into the first White House library. With the addition of her daughter's harp and piano, the room became a cozy place to entertain small groups of friends. It was in this room that Abigail spent her happiest hours, engaged in pleasant discourse with

OPPOSITE, LEFT: *Abigail Fillmore took an active interest in politics and, having been a teacher, appreciated intellectual guests. In many ways, she was a progressive woman; however, she demonstrated little interest in the emerging movement for women's rights.*

OPPOSITE, RIGHT: *Abigail Fillmore enjoyed selecting books for the first White House library. Among the hundreds of volumes she chose were biographies, history books, religious works, law books, travel books, and novels, including ones by Charles Dickens and William Thackeray.*

LEFT: *Abigail Fillmore wore this lavender silk gown when she was first lady of the nation. The dress features a gathered bodice that is complemented by a delicate embroidered shawl.*

JANE MEANS APPLETON PIERCE

March 12, 1806–December 2, 1863
Franklin Pierce, president 1853–1857

"I have known many of the ladies of the White House, none more truly excellent than the afflicted wife of President Pierce. Her health was a bar to any great effort on her part to meet the expectations of the public in her high position but she was a refined, extremely religious and well educated lady."

—Mrs. Robert E. Lee

*J*ane Appleton, born in Hampton, New Hampshire, in 1806, was the daughter of Jesse Appleton—a Congregational minister and president of Bowdoin College—and Elizabeth Means. When Jane was thirteen, her father died. She and her mother then moved to Amherst, New Hampshire, where they lived with Jane's wealthy maternal grandparents. Jane received an excellent education, with an emphasis on morality and divine wisdom. In 1826 she met Franklin Pierce, son of the governor of New Hampshire, and began seeing him socially. Jane's family was not pleased with the relationship. They knew that Franklin had political ambitions, and they did not consider politics a respectable occupation. Another concern was that Franklin suffered from periodic bouts of depression and was notorious for drinking too much. Despite her family's objections, on November 19, 1834, after a six-year engagement, Jane Appleton—a delicate, serious, deeply religious, melancholy young woman who suffered from recurrent attacks of tuberculosis—and Franklin Pierce—an outgoing, popular, newly elected congressman—were married.

From the beginning of their marriage, Franklin hired people to take care of the housework for his frail wife. After two terms in the House of Representatives, he was elected to the Senate. Living in Washington was torture for Jane. She detested the constant political talk and resented her husband's participation in rowdy after-hours parties with other elected officials, during which he drank excessively. Preferring private life, she was never supportive of her husband's political career. Jane found Washington to be depressing and unpleasant, and she refused to attend any social gatherings. In 1842, under pressure from his wife, Franklin resigned his Senate seat and promised to give up politics permanently. The family relocated to Concord, New Hampshire.

Jane was happy in Concord until two of her three sons died. The first son lived only a few days, and the second son died of typhus at the age of four. After their deaths, Jane focused all her attention on her only surviving child, Benjamin, known as "Bennie." In addition to Bennie's academic lessons, Jane made sure he received thorough religious training, which included daily family worship, listening to Bible stories, attending weekly church services, and hymn singing. While in Concord, the family worshiped at the Congregational church; in Washington, they attended the National Presbyterian Church.

In 1852—despite his promise to give up politics, and his wife's strong objections and ill health—Franklin Pierce accepted the nomination for the presidency. Jane was devastated when he won the election that November, but she reluctantly

made plans to move back to Washington. Only two months before Franklin was sworn in as America's fourteenth president, the family of three boarded a train in Andover, Massachusetts. Soon after the train left the station, their car derailed and tumbled down an embankment. Helpless, Jane and Franklin watched in horror as their eleven-year-old son was crushed to death beneath the train's wheels. The death of Bennie, their last child, was more than Jane could bear. Both parents were inconsolable: Jane felt that God had taken Bennie to keep Franklin from being distracted from his duties as president,

ABOVE: Jane Pierce's time in the White House was filled with grief and despair over the loss of her son Bennie. In a desperate attempt to contact the deceased child, the first lady called on the famous mediums the Fox Sisters to conduct a séance at the White House. Bennie's gravestone reads: "A loved and precious treasure lost to us here but safe in the Redeemer's care."

RIGHT: *During her time in the White House, Jane Pierce wore mourning attire. This particular dress has a black moiré foundation and an over-lay of black tulle embroidered with silver tinsel.*

hostess duties to her aunt Abby Means and her friend Mrs. Jefferson Davis, wife of the secretary of war.

After two years, the despondent first lady became known as "the Shadow of the White House." She ultimately forced herself to attend a small number of scheduled social functions and preside at a few state dinners. At receptions and the traditional New Year's Day open house, she stood beside her husband, looking forlorn in black mourning clothes. The guests would file by the president and first lady and then mingle in the East Room, but they were not offered any refreshments. Charles Mason, the commissioner of patents, said, "Everything in that mansion seems cold and cheerless. I have seen hundreds of log cabins which seemed to contain more happiness." Without a doubt, the socially starved Washingtonians endured a dark and depressing White House for four years. Even the state dinners had a restrained air, heightened by the fact that the president had given up wine and become a leader of the temperance movement.

LEFT: *Like his mother, Bennie Pierce did not want his father to become president. A year before his father was elected, Bennie wrote to his mother saying, "I hope he won't be elected for I should not like to be at Washington and I know you would not either."*

and Franklin felt that Bennie's death was retribution for his own shortcomings.

Jane did not attend her husband's inauguration, and there was no inaugural ball. Not being able to bear the thought of living in Washington without Bennie, Jane spent the first six months of her husband's administration in Baltimore. When the grief-stricken first lady finally moved into the White House, she stayed upstairs in the oval sitting room, writing letters to her dead son. Jane received relatives and friends, including her husband's former classmate Nathaniel Hawthorne, but rarely went downstairs or left the White House except to attend church services. She left most of the necessary

Jane was relieved to be out of the White House at the conclusion of her husband's term. She and Franklin then traveled throughout the Caribbean, hoping to find a climate better suited to her poor health. Wherever they traveled, Jane carried Bennie's Bible and a lock of his hair. She died in Andover at the age of fifty-seven and was buried next to Bennie.

HARRIET LANE

May 9, 1830–July 3, 1903
James Buchanan, president 1857–1861

"Low necks and lace berthas, made fashionable because of their adoption by Miss Lane, were worn almost universally....Jewels were conspicuous even in men's dressing, and gentlemen of fashion were rare who did not have varieties of sparkling studs and cravat-pins to add to the brightness of their vari-colored vests."

—Mrs. Clement Clay

OPPOSITE: *Harriet Lane spent mornings with her uncle President James Buchanan reading newspapers and discussing politics. The president respected her opinion and allowed Harriet to attend his cabinet meetings.*

After the death of her parents, eleven-year-old Harriet Lane asked if her uncle James Buchanan, then a senator from Pennsylvania, could be her guardian. When he received word of her request, Buchanan—despite the fact that he was a bachelor—replied that he would be very pleased to assume the responsibility of bringing up "this mischievous romp of a niece."

Born in Mercersburg, Pennsylvania, Harriet was the youngest daughter of James Buchanan's

sister, Jane, and Elliot Lane. Although Harriet was devastated over the death of her parents, she was pleased to be living with her uncle, whom she lovingly referred to as "Nunc." She attended boarding school in Pennsylvania, but summers and vacations were spent with her devoted uncle in Washington. The future president spoiled her so much during the times that they were together that her school's director sent a letter requesting that Harriet not spend vacations with him because the discipline that the teachers tried to instill in her was ruined by his indulgences.

Harriet grew into a well-educated, sophisticated young woman who moved comfortably in the social circles of both Washington and London, where her uncle served as minister to Great Britain. Queen Victoria was enchanted by Harriet and honored the girl with a status equivalent to that of ambassador's wife. By the time Buchanan entered the White House in 1857 as America's fifteenth president, Harriet was a polished twenty-six-year-old, ready to take on the duties of first lady. Her youthful exuberance and refined manner brought a cheerful tone and celebratory spirit back to the White House. After enduring the dismal days of the Pierce administration, Washington society was thrilled to welcome the vibrant new first lady. President Buchanan, too, enjoyed the social aspect of the White House. Only a few weeks into his presidency, he sent a note to the liquor merchants complaining about the small size of the champagne bottles being sent and explaining that "pints are very inconvenient as the article is not used in such small quantities." Buchanan was also particular about the quality of his food and regularly had fresh butter sent to the White House in a sealed brass kettle.

As the conflict heightened between the North and the South and war seemed inevitable, Harriet tried to maintain diplomacy during White House gatherings by forbidding any political talk during dinners. She also was careful not to sit political enemies next to one another. Harriet presided over several small weekly dinners as well as a weekly state dinner for forty, which included members of Congress and the Supreme Court, as well as other important guests. One day a week she held a drawing room, at which Washington ladies were careful

to take note of her attire so that they could copy her low necklines and full-hooped skirts. During the traditional New Year's Day open house, Harriet chose not to stand in the receiving line but rather stationed herself a distance away, posing with a bouquet of flowers and surrounded by her friends. Meanwhile, the president, rather than allowing the usual crush of people, greeted guests according to their rank. The vice president was first at 11:00 A.M., followed by the Speaker of the House, the cabinet, the Diplomat Corps, the Supreme Court, various military officers and other government officials, and finally, at noon, the general public.

Harriet made her mark on the White House in a number of ways. She promoted culture by inviting performers to give concerts at the Executive Mansion. To ensure that the building would be regularly filled with flowers, she saw to

MISS HARRIET LANE, THE PRESIDING LADY OF THE WHITE HOUSE.—From a Photograph.—See Page 283.

it that a greenhouse was built on the grounds of the Executive Mansion. She also bought elaborately carved plush chairs and sofas, upholstered in blue, for the Blue Room.

A highly popular first lady, Harriet Lane was bestowed with many honors. "Harriet" became the most popular name for newborn girls during her time in the White House, and composer Septimus Winner, also known as Alice Hawthorne, dedicated his song "Listen to the Mockingbird" to Harriet. The U.S. Coast Guard commissioned a steamship, the SS *Harriet Lane*, in 1858. (In 1982, a second U.S. Coast Guard ship was named the SS *Harriet Lane*, which continues in service today.) Harriet herself earned the respectful title "Great Mother," due to the compassion she demonstrated toward Native Americans when a Chippewa leader asked her to help stop the exploitation of his people by dishonest federal agents.

In 1860, Harriet presided over two noteworthy social events. That May, a Japanese delegation visiting America for the first time was received. Known for their strict adherence to protocol, the Japanese ambassadors felt that the only women of sufficiently high enough rank to be presented to them were the cabinet wives and Miss Lane. The Japanese presented twenty-eight boxes of gifts that included screens, kimonos, a tea set inlaid with pearls, and a cabinet that would stay on display in the White House's Green Room for nearly half a century. In October, Queen Victoria's son, the Prince of Wales, later to become King Edward VII, visited the White House, where he was honored with a state dinner. While in Washington, the prince made a special visit to Mount Vernon, where he laid a wreath on the grave of George Washington.

In 1861, when Buchanan's administration ended, Harriet and her uncle returned to Wheatland, his estate near Lancaster, Pennsylvania. On January 11,

1866, when she was thirty-five years old, Harriet Lane married Henry Elliott Johnston, a Baltimore banker. The couple became the parents of two sons, both of whom died of rheumatic fever as teenagers. In 1884, two years after the death of her second son, her husband died of pneumonia. On July 3, 1903, at the age of seventy-three, Harriet Lane Johnston succumbed to cancer. She bequeathed to the government her expansive art collection, which became the nucleus for the National Gallery of Art. She also founded the Harriet Lane Home for Invalid Children at Johns Hopkins University Hospital in Baltimore, which today is a highly regarded pediatric research facility.

BELOW: *Harriet Lane had this round divan situated in the center of the Blue Room in the White House. The plush furnishing was joined by eighteen other gilded pieces covered in blue brocatelle to form a conversation area. Made in Philadelphia by Gottlieb Vollmer, the pieces were reupholstered over the years in various shades of blue until they were finally replaced in 1902.*

MARY TODD LINCOLN

December 13, 1818–July 16, 1882
Abraham Lincoln, president 1861–1865

"I must dress in costly materials. The people scrutinize every article that I wear with critical curiosity."

—Mary Lincoln

At the age of eight, the ambitious Mary Ann Todd declared that when she grew up, she would marry the president and live in the White House. The fifth child of Eliza Ann Parker and Robert Smith Todd—a wealthy Lexington, Kentucky, banker—Mary was only seven when her mother died. A year later, her father remarried a woman who bore him nine more children. Todd provided his sons and daughters with all the material comforts they could want, but this did not quiet the explosive temper of the willful Mary, who never got along with her stepmother. Rather than live at home, the spirited young girl chose to attend boarding school. Sent to the finest private schools, she received an outstanding education and was taught social skills as well as French. She even impressed a friend of her father, Kentucky senator Henry Clay, with her knowledge of politics.

At the age of twenty-one, Mary Ann Todd moved to Springfield, Illinois, where she lived with her sister Elizabeth and brother-in-law Ninian Edwards. The Edwards household was a lively place where parties and dances were frequent events. At these gatherings, the witty, fashionable Mary Todd became the center of attention, attracting many suitors anxious for her hand in marriage.

It was at one of these parties that she met the tall, lanky country lawyer Abraham Lincoln. Although he was beneath her socially, Mary saw potential in the easygoing, intellectual lawyer and agreed to see him. Their courtship—which lasted three years—was volatile, and at one point, Lincoln broke off their engagement. Ultimately they reconciled, marrying on November 4, 1842.

During the couple's years in Springfield, Mary gave birth to four sons, one of whom died at the age of four. Not used to hard work, Mary had a difficult time adjusting to domestic life. The temper tantrums she threw often forced her husband and sons out of the house. But Abraham wasn't the only one who had to combat the emotional issues of a spouse. Mary herself had to learn to deal with Abraham's bouts of depression.

Despite their difficulties, Mary took great pride in Abraham as he built his name recognition with his legal practice, a term of service in Congress, and the debates with Stephen Douglas. In 1860, she was delighted to learn that her husband was the Republican nominee for president. When Abraham won the election, Mary's childhood dream of living in the White House was realized. On March 4, 1861, Abraham Lincoln was sworn in as America's sixteenth president—only one month before the first shots were fired on Fort Sumter, South Carolina, beginning a war that would tear the nation apart.

While Mary was all set to start her reign as the queen of Washington society, the citizens of the nation's capital were unwilling to accept her. Many people boycotted the inaugural ball and her first few receptions. She was accused of being a crude, ignorant hillbilly and a southern spy. In fact, nothing could have been further from the truth. In public, Mary was articulate, charming, and poised. However,

her critics continued to find fault with her. Anxious to please everyone—and to accommodate her own love of parties—Mary became determined to make the White House the social center of Washington.

However, the first lady quickly learned that when it came to pleasing the public, she couldn't win. If she entertained or spent money on clothes, she was rebuked for not caring about the Union soldiers. If she didn't entertain, she was criticized for not keeping up the morale of the country. In February 1862, when her eleven-year-old son, William, died from typhoid, Mary was criticized for purchasing

ABOVE: *Mary Lincoln became first lady only a month before the beginning of the Civil War. A staunch supporter of equality, she was the first of the nation's first ladies to invite black people into the White House as visitors. This photograph was created by Mathew B. Brady.*

ABOVE: *This painting depicts a young Mary Ann Todd at the time of her wedding. Once married, Mary wore a gold wedding band engraved with the words, "Love is Eternal."*

OPPOSITE: *Mary Lincoln bought this bed for a White House guest room. Although President Lincoln never slept in the bed, it has come to be known as the Lincoln bed.*

too much, became jealous of any woman who was around her husband, suffered from migraine headaches, and often shouted at anyone in sight. Her tendency toward impulsive shopping sprees worsened as retailers gladly gave her credit. Without her husband's knowledge, Mary ran up a $27,000 bill at a New York department store.

Despite her huge debts, her mental condition, and the barrage of criticism, Mary still enjoyed the spotlight and presided over numerous state dinners and receptions. She also did her part to help out with the war. As the number of casualties grew, she rolled bandages, visited injured soldiers in hospitals, and accompanied her husband when he reviewed troops in the field. Furthermore, she freely gave input on the president's choice of generals and discussed military campaigns with him.

When Congress appropriated $20,000 to refurbish the White House, Mary personally supervised the cleaning, painting, and redecorating. She purchased plush carpeting, furniture, and thick lace curtains typical of the Victorian era. A substantial amount of money was spent on redecorating one of the guest bedrooms, which she had wallpapered and furnished with an eight-foot (2.4m)-long, ornately carved rosewood bed. This bed, which came to be known as the Lincoln bed, remains in the White House today. She also made good use of the new conservatory, filling the White House with plants and flowers. Even her critics were impressed by the new look.

Mary was elated when her husband was reelected in 1864. After the inauguration, the president and first lady received fifteen thousand visitors offering congratulations. At the inaugural ball, held at the Patent Office, Mary Todd Lincoln wore a white silk gown that cost $2,000. Scarcely a month later, on April 14, 1865, the president was shot at Ford's Theatre.

Mary was too distraught to attend her husband's funeral. Despondent and confused, she took nearly

expensive mourning clothes. Willie's death devastated the Lincolns, and Mary nearly suffered a nervous breakdown. She spent days refusing to get out of bed and experienced visions of Willie talking to her. She even hired a spiritualist to conduct séances in the hope of communicating with her cherished son. Despite the fact that she was suffering through an extremely painful period, critics continued to attack Mary, accusing her of neglecting her duties as first lady by cutting back on her social responsibilities.

The constant criticism contributed to the deterioration of Mary's mental stability. She ate

RIGHT: *Adorned with woven purple flowers and black stripes, this off-white silk taffeta gown worn by Mary Lincoln features a day bodice. A matching evening bodice was worn off the shoulders.*

four months to move out of the White House. During this time, the general public had practically open access to the building, where they freely helped themselves to souvenirs. People took china, silver, and furniture; they even cut off pieces of curtains, carpets, and wallpaper. The mansion that had received rave reviews after Mrs. Lincoln's redecorating effort was now in shambles.

In 1868, Mary and her youngest son, Thomas (called "Tad"), left for Europe, where they traveled extensively. Sadly, in 1871, Tad died after a short bout of the flu. The death of her youngest son seemed to push Mary to the breaking point. Robert Todd Lincoln, her only surviving son, recognized that she needed psychological help, and in 1875 he had her committed to a mental institution. Mary was released within a year, at which point she returned to her sister's house in Springfield. She died in relative obscurity in 1882 at the age of sixty-three in her sister's home.

ABOVE: *This painting by Francis B. Carpenter shows President Lincoln with his wife, Mary, and their three sons—Robert, Willie, and Tad. Mary and Abraham Lincoln were tolerant parents who rarely reprimanded their children.*

ELIZA MCCARDLE JOHNSON

October 4, 1810–January 15, 1876
Andrew Johnson, president 1865–1869

"I do not like this public life at all. I often wish the time would come when we could
return to where I feel we best belong."

—*Eliza Johnson*

Eliza McCardle, born in Leesburg, Tennessee, was the only child of Sarah Phillips and John McCardle. After John died during Eliza's early childhood, her mother supported the small family by making quilts and renting out rooms. Although they lived on limited means, Eliza was able to attend Rhea Academy in Greeneville, Tennessee, where she received a basic education. Eliza met Andrew Johnson in September 1826, when he moved to Greeneville with his mother and step-father. The following spring, on May 17, 1827, eighteen-year-old Andrew Johnson and sixteen-year-old Eliza McCardle were married. Over the years, the couple would become the parents of five children.

The newlyweds set up housekeeping in a two-room home in Greeneville. In the front parlor, Andrew established a tailor shop, where Eliza kept him company by reading, tutoring him in math, and teaching him to write. (Because of his family's extreme poverty, Andrew had not received a for-mal education, though he had taught himself how to read.) Andrew was ambitious and rose rapidly in politics, serving as a representative in the state legislature, as a U.S. congressman, as governor of Tennessee, and as a U.S. senator. At the beginning

of the Civil War, he was appointed military governor of Tennessee with headquarters in Nashville. Eliza stayed in Greeneville until Jefferson Davis imposed martial law in eastern Tennessee, which had remained loyal to the Union. When the Confederates confiscated their property, Eliza was given thirty-six hours to vacate her home. It was months before she was able to join her husband in Nashville.

During the campaign of 1864, incumbent President Abraham Lincoln dropped his previous vice president, Hannibal Hamlin, and replaced him with Andrew Johnson. With Lincoln's successful reelection, Johnson became the new vice president. In March 1865, when Andrew left for Washington to take the oath of office, Eliza stayed home in Nashville. Little more than a month later, after the death of Abraham Lincoln, Andrew Johnson became president of the United States.

The Johnson family was sympathetic to Lincoln's widow and never made her feel rushed to vacate the Executive Mansion. In August, Eliza and the new president moved into the White House with their two sons; their widowed daughter, Mary Stover, and her two children; and another daughter and son-in-law, Martha and David Patterson, and

ABOVE: *Eliza Johnson showed little interest in politics but steadfastly supported her husband during his impeachment proceedings. Quiet and reserved, she had a calming influence on her easily upset husband.*

Eng.d by J.C.Buttre.

ABOVE: *Although it was a strain to be in the public eye, Martha Johnson Patterson admirably filled in as first lady for her ailing mother. Martha once remarked to a reporter, "If I could only walk about a little with my children sometimes in the grounds without being stared at, and really enjoy the comfort of an old dress and a little privacy, it would be very pleasant."*

the necessary repairs had been completed and the furniture replaced, the total cost came to more than $130,000.

During her husband's administration, Eliza stayed in a room on the second floor, where she read, sewed, and enjoyed her grandchildren. She made only two public appearances during her husband's term. The first occurred in August 1866 during the visit of Hawaii's Queen Emma. The second was in December 1868 on the occasion of her husband's sixtieth birthday, which they celebrated by inviting children living in Washington to a "children's ball," held in the East Room. At both of these events, Eliza remained seated, explaining to the guests that she was an invalid.

Unostentatious, Martha Patterson deftly entertained in such a way that put both the social elite of Washington and ordinary citizens at ease. She stated, "We are a plain people from the mountains of Tennessee called here for a short time by a national calamity. I trust too much will not be expected of us." Martha dutifully presided as White House hostess at state dinners and held a regular Monday afternoon drawing room. Her competence and unpretentious style soothed uncomfortable politicians during her father's impeachment proceedings in 1868, when charges were brought against him by Republican radicals who were angered by his compassionate policies toward the South during Reconstruction. President Johnson was acquitted when Congress was unable to obtain the necessary two-thirds majority vote needed for impeachment.

their three children. Eliza was almost fifty-five years old and suffering from tuberculosis when she became first lady. Because her treatment required her to rest and stay indoors, she depended upon her daughter Martha to serve as White House hostess.

When the Johnsons moved into the Executive Mansion, they found that the building had been ravaged. Immediately after Lincoln's assassination, throngs of people had descended upon the White House to take prized souvenirs. Congress appropriated $30,000 for cleanup, renovation, and refurbishing, but it was soon apparent that this amount of money was not going to be enough. When all

At the end of Johnson's term, Eliza was happy to return to her home in Tennessee, which had been repaired after the war. In 1874, her husband was elected to the U.S. Senate, but he served only briefly, dying shortly after taking office. Eliza died less than six months after her husband at the home of her daughter Martha.

LEFT: *Martha Johnson Patterson wore this hooded opera cloak, or burnoose, over a brocade gown. The burnoose is made of finely woven wool adorned with gold braiding and tassels.*

JULIA DENT GRANT

January 26, 1826–December 14, 1902

Ulysses S. Grant, president 1869–1877

"Eight happy years I spent there. So happy! It still seems as much like home to me as the old farm in Missouri."

—Julia Grant reflecting upon her time in the White House

Julia Boggs Dent was born at White Haven, her family's plantation, near St. Louis, Missouri. She was the daughter of Ellen Wrenshall and Frederick Dent, the latter a wealthy planter who provided his children with all the comforts and educational opportunities available. In the spring of 1844, Julia's brother Frederick introduced her to Ulysses Grant, his West Point roommate. Grant found the outspoken, plain-looking, cross-eyed eighteen-year-old to be enchanting. For him it was love at first sight. The two became engaged immediately, though they weren't married until four years later, on August 22, 1848, after Grant's service

in the Mexican War. Both families were against the marriage. Julia's father didn't want her to wed a career military officer, and Grant's opposed the union because the Dents were slaveholders.

Military life was difficult for Ulysses. As a devoted husband and father, he missed being with his wife and children and started drinking heavily. In 1854, he resigned his commission. He tried to make a living in other occupations such as farming and real estate but was unsuccessful. In 1861, with the outbreak of the Civil War, he was appointed colonel and soon after became a general. Whenever possible, Julia accompanied him to his encampments, where she tended to the wounded, wrote letters for the soldiers, and readily gave her opinions regarding her husband's planned military maneuvers. At the end of the war, the successful, immensely popular hero was appointed general of the army, then acting secretary of war. In 1868, he was elected president of the United States.

Grant, who had never had any interest in politics, had sought the presidency for one reason: to please his ambitious wife. On March 4, 1869, immediately after taking the oath of office, the new president turned to his wife and said, "Well, my dear, I hope now you are satisfied."

Ulysses, Julia, and the younger two of their four children, as well as Julia's father, entered the White House at the beginning of America's opulent Gilded Age. Julia accepted expensive gifts from friends, wore fashionable clothes and costly jewels, and entertained luxuriously. The rich postwar society welcomed the grandeur and, in contrast to the public's response toward Mary Todd Lincoln, praised Mrs. Grant for her extravagance. In the White House, Julia added plush furnishings, gilded wallpaper, and other ornate Victorian embellishments. False beams were added to the East Room ceiling, splitting it into three sections. In each section hung an $1,800 chandelier adorned with thousands of pieces of cut glass. Outside, Julia had the White House gates closed so that she and her children could enjoy the grounds peacefully without being followed by throngs of people.

In addition to hosting state dinners and the Fourth of July and New Year's Day open houses, the first lady also held Tuesday and Saturday receptions, often inviting cabinet wives to join her in the receiving line. She presided over lavish twenty-nine-course dinners, which usually featured six different wines. Even though the state dining room

seated only thirty-six people at that time, dinners could cost as much as $2,000.

Julia's father, "Colonel Dent," was a conspicuous presence at the White House during the Grant administration. He voiced his opinion on everything from the china pattern Julia had selected to politics, freely sharing his observations with anyone waiting to see the president. During Julia's drawing rooms, her father sat in a chair in the Blue Room, where guests were expected to greet him ahead of his daughter.

Without doubt, the Grants entertained elaborately, but nothing compared to the May 1874 fairy-tale wedding of their nineteen-year-old daughter,

ABOVE: *Julia Grant had dark hair, brown eyes, and a plump figure. Though she was considered plain-looking, her energetic personality charmed nearly everyone.*

When she discovered that her husband had written a note to the Republican party declining to run for a third term, she became furious and demanded to know why he hadn't shown her the correspondence. He replied, "My dear, if I had shown you the note it would never have been sent."

Julia officiated as White House hostess for the last time when she gave a post-inaugural luncheon for President and Mrs. Hayes, thus ending what Julia referred to as the happiest period in her life. Julia and Ulysses left immediately on a two-year tour around the world. Upon their return, the former president learned he was dying from throat cancer. In order to ensure his wife's financial security, he worked feverishly to write his memoirs, finishing only days before his death on July 23, 1885. Seventeen years later, Julia died at the age of seventy-six. Their joint gravesite, "Grant's Tomb," is a popular New York City tourist attraction.

ABOVE: *This Grant family portrait depicts, from left to right: Jesse (the youngest son), Ulysses Jr. (known as Buck), Nellie (in back), Frederick (the oldest son), Julia, and Ulysses Grant.*

RIGHT: *After the death of President Grant, American citizens donated more than $600,000 for the construction of his tomb. The memorial ultimately became the final resting place for both the former president and his wife. Located in New York City, the granite-and-marble structure is the largest mausoleum in North America.*

Nellie. The bride wore a $5,000 wedding dress and was married in the East Room in front of two hundred invitees. After the ceremony, the guests were treated to a twenty-seven-course luncheon. The gifts that poured in from all over the country and around the world were valued at more than $75,000. In addition, the president and first lady presented the bride with a diamond necklace and earrings, plus a check for $10,000.

Julia immensely enjoyed her tenure as first lady. She was popular and very much politically involved with her husband. She advised him on cabinet appointments, attended cabinet and Senate meetings, met with justices and diplomats, and read the president's mail. Despite the fact that Grant's administration was marked by scandals and many of his appointees were corrupt men who took advantage of him, Julia did not want to leave the White House.

LEFT: *This silk evening gown was worn by Julia Grant. The damask fabric features a rose pattern highlighted with silver thread.*

LUCY WARE WEBB HAYES

August 28, 1831–June 25, 1889
Rutherford B. Hayes, president 1877–1881

"A woman's mind is as strong as a man's, equal in all things and is superior in some."

—*Lucy Hayes*

Lucy Ware Webb was the youngest of three children of Dr. James Webb and Maria Cook of Chillicothe, Ohio. After her father's death, Lucy, her mother, and her two brothers relocated to Delaware, Ohio. In 1850, Lucy graduated from Wesleyan Female College in Cincinnati, making her the first of the nation's first ladies to earn a college degree.

Maria Webb and her friend Sophia Hayes, also a widow, decided that their children would make a good couple and set about playing matchmaker. Lucy and Rutherford heard a lot about each other before they finally met. When they did become acquainted, Rutherford was impressed with not only Lucy's intelligence but her beauty, making entries in his diary about her rich brown eyes and

low, sweet voice. On December 30, 1852, after a five-year courtship, the two were married at the Cincinnati home of Lucy's mother. The couple became the parents of eight children, three of whom died in infancy.

During the Civil War, like many other women, Lucy joined her husband as often as possible at his military posts, throughout his rise from major to general. She was held in high esteem by the men under her husband's command, who called her "Mother Hayes." After the war, Rutherford Hayes was elected to Congress, later becoming governor of Ohio. Aware that her roles of mother and wife were both important, Lucy balanced raising a family with supporting her husband's career. She traveled with Rutherford throughout Ohio and was sensitive to the needs of the state's citizens. When she learned that the state legislature refused to appropriate funds to provide a home for war orphans, Lucy and her friends collected voluntary contributions to build one.

Early in life Lucy had been influenced by abolitionists and political reformers, as well as by her education and strict Methodist upbringing. While she was a supporter of the early feminist movement, which demanded equal pay for women, she was against women having the right to vote. When her husband became a presidential candidate in 1876, she earned the reputation of a woman who could speak intelligently about politics. On March 5, 1877, after a bitterly contested election that was finally decided by an electoral commission, Rutherford Hayes became the nation's nineteenth president.

Lucy Hayes came into the White House during a time when women's organizations were beginning to redefine a woman's role in America. During this postwar period, women were starting to become more focused on social reform and volunteer groups. National organizations such as the YWCA and the Women's Christian Temperance Union—which promoted the legal ban of alcohol—were forming. Although the first lady felt that alcohol consumption should be a personal decision, her husband believed that alcohol was a bad influence on his sons—and his country—and banned it from the White House. When Washington society learned of this ban, Mrs. Hayes' name was swept into the forefront of the temperance movement, resulting in her being labeled with the nickname "Lemonade Lucy."

Although entertaining was by no means minimal, the administration was considered serene by

comparison to the excesses that had pervaded Grant's term. Twice daily, the Hayeses had family devotions; nearly every evening, they received visitors; and on Sunday evenings, members of the cabinet and Congress were invited to sing hymns. In addition to private, informal entertaining, there were the customary luncheons, open houses, and elaborate state dinners. To enhance the White House dining experience, Mrs. Hayes commissioned a unique thousand-piece dinner service depicting America's flora and fauna in twelve different designs. The most elaborate social occasion during Rutherford Hayes' term was the celebration of the presidential couple's twenty-fifth wedding

ABOVE: *Lucy Hayes was the first of America's first ladies to graduate from college. Women reformers asked her to speak out on behalf of suffrage and higher education for women, but she refused.*

anniversary, during which husband and wife renewed their vows.

Other events were geared toward recognizing the hard work of the White House staff. Every Thanksgiving Day, staff members and their families were invited to a dinner, followed by games in the Red Room. At Christmas, the staff was given a party and gifts were personally selected by Mrs. Hayes. These presents were cheerfully handed to the intended recipients by Lucy and Rutherford's two youngest children, Scott and

Fannie, who were eight and ten years old, respectively, when they moved into the White House. The Hayeses delighted in being around children. When Lucy found out that the annual Easter Egg Roll on the Capitol grounds was being discontinued because congressmen had complained of slipping on the eggshell remains, she invited the children of Washington to use the South Lawn of the White House. This Easter Monday tradition grew more popular every year and continues to thrive today.

LEFT: *The invention of the sewing machine encouraged designers to create dresses that were more elaborate. This machine-made gown worn by Lucy Hayes at two White House functions is heavily ornamented with pleats, ruffles, and fringe.*

RIGHT: *When publications such as* **Harper's Weekly** *and* **Frank Leslie's Illustrated Newspaper** *began to chronicle the lives of America's first ladies, their female readership increased. Details regarding Lucy Hayes' clothing, personality, and conduct were printed often.*

OPPOSITE: *Designed by American artist Theodore Russell Davis and produced by Haviland and Company, the Hayes state dinner and dessert service bears depictions of American plants and animals, including okra, corn, turkeys, buffalo, fish, and antelope, some of which are shown here. Notice the ice cream plate (center row, left), which features a snowshoe. The set was first put to use in 1880 at a celebration for president-elect James Garfield.*

The president respected Lucy's mind and keen political intellect. It was implied that she had a great deal of influence with her husband, and he often sought her counsel before instituting matters of public policy. In March 1878, when the first lady made a brief trip outside Washington without her husband, the *Boston Post* quipped, "During the absence of Mrs. Hayes, Mr. Hayes will be the acting president."

The White House played host to numerous historic events during the Hayeses' time there. April 1878 brought new technology into the mansion when Thomas Edison demonstrated the phonograph to President and Mrs. Hayes, and Alexander Graham Bell instructed them in the use of the telephone. In November 1878, the world-famous soprano Maria Selika, known as the "Queen of Staccato," sang at the White House, making her the first black artist ever to perform there. In 1880, Queen Victoria presented the president with a desk made from the British ship *Resolute*. This desk would be used by nearly every president thereafter and has become one of the most famous pieces of furniture in the White House.

After President Hayes' term was over, Lucy became involved with the Woman's Home Missionary Society of the Methodist Episcopal Church, which looked after poor women and female immigrants. She died of a stroke two months before her fifty-eighth birthday. In the 1881 edition of *Ladies of the White House*, author Laura Holloway wrote of Mrs. Hayes, "Her strong, healthful influence gives the world assurances of what the next century's women will be."

LUCRETIA RUDOLPH GARFIELD

April 19, 1832–March 14, 1918
James A. Garfield, president 1881

"We should remember greatness is not in station, but as is often said,
'Act well your part, there all honor lies.'"

—*Lucretia Garfield*

*L*ucretia Rudolph, born in 1832 in Hiram, Ohio, was the daughter of Arabella Green Mason and Zebulon Rudolph, the latter a carpenter, part-time preacher, and cofounder of the Eclectic Institute at Hiram. "Crete," as she was known to her family and friends, met James Garfield at Geauga Seminary in Chester, Ohio. From there, both attended the Eclectic Institute. After graduation, Lucretia began teaching school and James continued his education at Williams College in Williamstown, Massachusetts. While Lucretia was plain-looking, reserved, unaffectionate, and often ill, James was sociable and demonstrative. Despite their personality differences, they were married on November 11, 1858. Bride and groom were both twenty-six years old.

James Garfield considered going into the ministry but decided instead to pursue a career in education. After teaching classical languages and becoming president of the Eclectic Institute, he gave up academics to enter politics. In 1859, he was elected to the Ohio state senate. At the outbreak of the Civil War, Garfield joined Ohio's Forty-second Regiment, advancing from lieutenant colonel to major general. In 1862, while still serving in the Union army, he was elected to Congress. In order to take the seat, he resigned his commission. At this point, his marriage to Lucretia was strained because he had been unfaithful to her during his time in the military, but she eventually forgave him and their union strengthened.

During James' tenure as a member of Congress, he and Lucretia chose not to participate in the parties of Washington's social set. The couple much preferred the company of their friends in the literary society to which they belonged, as well as evenings at home discussing news and politics and spending time with their young children. When incumbent President Rutherford B. Hayes kept his promise to the American people to serve only one term, the Republican committee nominated James Garfield as their presidential candidate. In the tight election of 1880, he defeated Civil War hero Winfield Scott Hancock by only ten thousand votes.

The newly elected president and his family, which included five highly active children ranging in ages from nine to eighteen (two children had previously died in infancy), moved into the White House in March 1881. As first lady, Mrs. Garfield held receptions twice a week. She also spent much time at the Library of Congress researching the history of the White House, which once again was badly in need of refurbishing. Her goal was to furnish the mansion with authentic pieces from previous administrations. Unfortunately, in May she developed a severe case of malaria, which nearly took her life. In order to escape the heat and humidity of Washington, Lucretia went to a seaside resort in Elberton, New Jersey, where she slowly recovered from her bout with malaria. While in Elberton, she received a telegram stating that her husband had been shot. She rushed back to Washington and, even though she was frail and fatigued, rarely left

her husband's side during the two months he lay dying. Lucretia's vision of a beautifully restored White House, in which all Americans could take pride, was cut short by the president's death on September 19, 1881. It would be eighty years before another first lady achieved that goal.

Following James Garfield's death, Congress bestowed on Lucretia an annual pension of $5,000.

ABOVE: *Lucretia Garfield was the second first lady to lose her husband to an assassin. When the president's body was being transported to the burial place in Ohio, Lucretia insisted that the curtains in the railroad car remain open.*

ABOVE: *President and Mrs. Garfield had their children take music and dance lessons. The president enjoyed listening to Hal, his eldest son, play a Bradbury upright piano that remains in the White House.*

A subscription in her support that was launched by financier Cyrus W. Field ultimately raised the impressive sum of $300,000. With this money, the former first lady was able to live comfortably for the remainder of her life. After donating her husband's papers to the Library of Congress,

Lucretia spent the rest of her thirty-six years between Lawnsfield, her Ohio estate, and her winter home in Pasadena, California, where she died at the age of eighty-five. Husband and wife are buried next to each other at Lakeview Cemetery in Cleveland, Ohio.

LEFT: *Lucretia Garfield wore this satin gown to the 1881 inaugural ball. Although the gown now appears to be cream-colored, the original hue was lavender. The fabric has faded because the dye used was light-sensitive.*

FRANCES FOLSOM CLEVELAND

July 21, 1864–October 29, 1947

Grover Cleveland, president 1885–1889 and 1893–1897

"I can wish the women of our country no greater blessing than that their homes and lives may be as happy, and their husbands may be as kind, attentive, considerate and affectionate as mine."

—Frances Cleveland, June 3, 1888

The Blue Room was an explosion of color. Palm trees nearly touched the ceiling. Garlands of greenery and roses adorned the chandeliers and mirrors, while red geraniums and white lilies set off the green foliage. On a far wall, yellow pansies wrote out the date: June 2, 1886. Thirty invited guests looked on while hundreds of people strained to see through the open windows. The Marine Corps Band, led by John Phillip Sousa, played as the twenty-one-year-old bride entered the room on the arm of her groom, the forty-nine-year-old president of the United States.

Born in Buffalo, New York, in 1864, Frances Folsom was the only child of Emma Cornelia Harmon and Oscar Folsom, the latter a close friend and law partner of Grover Cleveland. In fact, one of the baby's first gifts was a carriage bought by Cleveland. When Frances was only eleven, her father was killed in a wagon accident and Cleveland was named administrator of the Folsom estate. Frances and her mother remained close friends with Cleveland as he rose in politics from sheriff of Erie County to governor of New York and finally to the presidency. While "Frankie" was a student at Wells College, Cleveland kept her room filled with flowers. When word leaked out that the president was secretly engaged, speculation was that he would marry Mrs. Folsom. To the surprise of everyone, Cleveland announced that he was engaged to Frances.

Frances Folsom Cleveland was popular with the public from the beginning. Americans could not get enough news about the young first lady. While the newlyweds were on their honeymoon, reporters with field glasses spied on them. The press even bribed waiters going into the honeymoon cottage in order to obtain reports on the type of food being served. As first lady, Mrs. Cleveland presided over luncheons, teas, receptions, state dinners, and open houses. When she learned that employed women, called "shop girls," were unable to attend an open house during the week, she opened the White House on Saturday afternoon specifically to accommodate them. These receptions became so popular that thousands of people passed through the Executive Mansion wanting to shake hands with the charming first lady. Often, after these events, Mrs. Cleveland required massages to relieve the pain in her hands and arms.

In 1888, Grover Cleveland ran for reelection against Republican Benjamin Harrison. The opposition circulated stories that the Clevelands' marriage had failed and that the president got drunk, beat his wife, and threw her out of the house. Frances had little interest in politics, but because of the attack, she issued a press statement defending the president. This marked the first time that a first lady was forced to issue a press statement defending her husband and marriage. Despite Frances' efforts, Harrison defeated President Cleveland in the election. However, four years later Cleveland was again

elected president, making him the only chief executive to serve two nonconsecutive terms.

When Grover and Frances Cleveland returned to the White House in 1893, all was not the same as when they had left. First of all, a number of improvements, including the addition of electric lights, had been made to the building during the Harrison administration. Second, the Cleveland family now included a daughter, Ruth, who had been born in 1891. The young girl, affectionately called "Baby Ruth"—and for whom the Baby Ruth candy bar is supposedly named—was the darling of the American public. People visited the White House just hoping to get a glimpse of her.

ABOVE: *From the moment she entered the White House as President Cleveland's vivacious young bride, Frances Cleveland captured the interest—and the hearts—of the nation. The public could not get enough information about her, and the press was quick to capitalize on the demand.*

RIGHT: *Frances Folsom is pictured here in the dress she wore when she married President Grover Cleveland. The ivory satin gown was made in Paris. Orange blossoms edge the bodice and extend down the left side of the draped skirt, while smaller sprigs of these blooms adorn the three-quarter-length sleeves.*

BELOW: *The newlywed Clevelands gave each guest a lace-trimmed, satin-covered wedding cake box. Each box was signed by both the bride and groom.*

OPPOSITE: *Frances Cleveland wore her wedding gown on subsequent occasions and had the dress modified a number of times. In one incarnation, the original high neck was changed to a V-neck, and the orange blossoms and sleeves were removed. Later, a dickey was incorporated to fill in the low neckline and the sleeves were put back into place. It is this last version that is pictured here, though the dickey and one sleeve are reproductions.*

ABOVE: *This photograph shows Frances Cleveland relaxing in the White House. The sitting room—located at the west end of the open hallway on the second floor—was a favorite gathering place for the Clevelands.*

After one incident in which admirers pulled Ruth from her nurse's arms and passed her around the crowd, Mrs. Cleveland ordered the gates closed to protect her daughter. In September 1893, just six months after the Clevelands returned to the White House, another daughter, Esther, joined the growing family. The birth of Esther, the first child of a president to be born in the White House, delighted the public. During this time, the president secretly underwent surgery for mouth cancer in which part of his jaw was removed. However, news of Esther's birth so distracted the American public that the president's operation went completely unreported. In July 1895, during the family's summer vacation in Buzzard's Bay, Massachusetts, a third daughter, Marion, was born.

During Cleveland's second term in office, the entire family lived for most of the year in the Georgetown home they called "Woodley," located a few miles away from the White House, and the president commuted. This measure was designed to give the family some freedom from crowds and prying reporters. The Georgetown home, which sat on several acres, was surrounded by a fence and had a gatehouse, giving the Clevelands a sense of privacy, as well as security, for their children.

Between December and March, the busiest part of the social season in Washington, the Clevelands all resided at the White House. During Christmas 1895, much to the delight of their daughters, the Clevelands put up a tree decorated with an exciting modern invention: electric lights.

Frances did little entertaining during Christmas, devoting her time instead to working with a Washington charity that provided food, clothing, and toys to needy families.

After leaving the White House, the Clevelands moved to Princeton, New Jersey. In 1897, Frances gave birth to a son, Richard, and in 1903, their last child, Francis, was born. The Cleveland family divided their time between their residence in New Jersey and their summer home in New Hampshire. On June 24, 1908, after a long illness, the former president died. Five years later, in February 1913, Frances Cleveland married Thomas J. Preston, a professor of archaeology. The former first lady was active in the Women's University Club and many charitable organizations. She died in October 1947 at the age of eighty-three.

CAROLINE LAVINIA SCOTT HARRISON

October 1, 1832–October 25, 1892
Benjamin Harrison, president 1889–1893

"Since this Society has been organized and so much thought and reading directed to the early struggles of this country, it has been made plain that much of its success was due to the character of the women of that era. The unselfish part they acted constantly commends itself to our admiration and example."

—Caroline Harrison in an address to the Daughters of the American Revolution, February 22, 1892

Caroline Lavinia Scott was born in Oxford, Ohio, in October 1832. She was the daughter of Mary Neal and the Reverend John W. Scott, the latter a Presbyterian minister and educator. One of the reverend's students, Benjamin Harrison, became a frequent visitor to the family's home, where he met Caroline, who was attending the Oxford Female Institute. On October 20, 1853, Caroline and Benjamin were married at her parents' home, with her father performing the

ceremony. The couple eventually became the parents of three children, two of whom lived to maturity.

Benjamin Harrison gave serious thought to going into the ministry but decided instead on a law career. After being admitted to the bar, he set up a practice and worked long hours building up his reputation. He also became involved in Republican politics. During the Civil War, he joined the Union army as a second lieutenant in the Seventieth Indiana Volunteers, eventually becoming a brigadier general. After the war, Benjamin rose in the political ranks to become a U.S. senator and eventually, like his grandfather William Henry Harrison, the president of the United States.

In March 1889, the newly elected president and the first lady moved into the Executive Mansion, bringing with them Caroline's father, as well as Mary Dimmick, Caroline's young widowed niece, who acted as her social secretary. The Harrisons' daughter, Mary Harrison McKee, and her husband, James, also moved into the White House, along with their young children. The McKee children were a hit with the American public, especially two-year-old Benjamin, known as "Baby McKee." Newspapers were beginning to use photography, and pictures of the president's grandson sold papers. Caroline recognized her grandson's popularity and agreed to allow the press to take pictures of him once a week in exchange for leaving him alone the rest of the time. This began what is commonly known today as the photo op.

At the time that the Harrisons entered the White House, the structure was in desperate need of restoration. Feeling that the building was beyond repair, Mrs. Harrison thought that it should be torn down and a new one erected on the same site. Congress did not agree and instead appropriated $35,000 for refurbishing. Although disappointed, the new first lady set about her improvement project with vigor, commencing by having the building scoured from top to bottom and getting rid of a rat infestation. She personally oversaw all changes from the basement to the family quarters. The rotten kitchen floors on the ground level were replaced, rooms were repainted and re-wallpapered, and new draperies and furnishings were purchased. Each bedroom gained its own

separate bathroom, which improved the quality of living. The old conservatory was overhauled, and new greenhouses were added. On a technological note, a central switchboard was installed, which allowed for several telephone lines instead of just one. The biggest improvement came in 1891 with the installation of electric lights. But because the Harrisons were terrified of getting a shock from the light switches, they continued to use, for the most part, the old gaslights. Only when a staff

ABOVE: *Caroline Harrison enjoyed being involved, whether it was with her church, women's clubs, her local community, or the nation. She balanced taking care of her family and her home with her artwork, love of music, and passionate campaigning for social and women's causes.*

member was available to turn the electric lights on and off were they used. It was not uncommon for the lights to be left on all night until the engineer came in the next morning.

Caroline was a talented artist who enjoyed china painting. She brought her own kiln with her to the White House and taught china painting to the cabinet wives. This interest led her to design a new White House china pattern, which incorporated corn and goldenrod. After she came across collections of china from previous administrations, she had them put on display. This was the beginning of the White House china collection, which continues to be a popular tourist attraction.

As first lady, Caroline presided over receptions, open houses, and elegant state dinners, as well as smaller parties for family and friends. Christmas 1889 brought the first family Christmas tree into the White House. It was placed in the upstairs family living area. But Caroline did more than perform her entertaining responsibilities. Understanding the power of publicity associated with being the first lady, she used her highly visible position to help women's organizations. She donated her needlework to church bazaars and became the first president of the Daughters of the American Revolution. When the Johns Hopkins School of

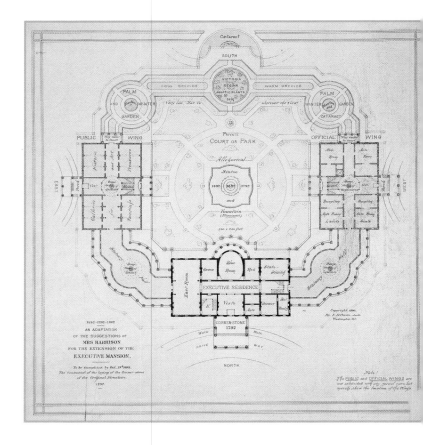

Medicine in Baltimore asked Mrs. Harrison for help raising funds, she agreed to do so on the condition that female students be admitted. With that assurance she gave her assistance, and the school raised $500,000.

During the summer of 1892, while her husband was campaigning for reelection, Caroline Harrison developed tuberculosis, a disease that led to her

death on October 25, only two weeks before Election Day. After she died, the president lost interest in campaigning. His opponent, former president Grover Cleveland, once again was elected chief executive. Caroline's funeral was held in the East Room, and after the official period of mourning ended, her daughter, Mrs. Mary McKee, acted as the nation's hostess for the remainder of her father's term.

Three years later, in April 1896, the sixty-two-year-old former president married his wife's thirty-seven-year-old niece, Mary Dimmick, who had lived in the White House with them. In 1897, they became the parents of a daughter.

IDA SAXTON MCKINLEY

June 8, 1847–May 26, 1907
William McKinley, president 1897–1901

"I must return to Mrs. McKinley at once. She is among strangers."

—President William McKinley to newspaper publisher H.H. Kohlsaat after a private meeting, April 1898

Ida Saxton was born to Catherine DeWalt and James Saxton, the latter a wealthy Canton, Ohio, banker. In 1869, after graduating from Brook Hall Seminary in Pennsylvania, Ida went with her sister on an eight-month grand tour of Europe. When Ida returned, she was expected to immerse herself in society functions, but instead she went to work as a cashier in her father's bank. William McKinley, a local Canton attorney who had risen to the rank of major during the Civil War, often brought Ida flowers at the bank. After their marriage on January 25, 1871, they moved into a large house on Market Street, a wedding gift from Ida's father. The couple became the parents of two daughters, but neither child lived long; ents of two daughters, but neither child lived long;

one died in infancy, and the other died of typhoid fever when she was only four years old.

Ida never recovered from the loss of her daughters. She became quarrelsome and suffered from migraine headaches. She may also have developed a mild form of epilepsy that kept her dependent on her husband, who selflessly catered to her every need and desire. Bromides for her indigestion and massages for her headaches lessened her pain, but she required constant attention and freedom from any source of stress.

William McKinley was devoted to his invalid wife. When he was unable to take care of her, he always hired someone to make sure that she was comfortable. Publicly, he minimized her poor health,

so few people realized how incapacitated she really was. In fact, his reticence about her condition sometimes led to misimpressions. His political opponents, for instance, accused him of having a domineering wife because he spent so much time by her side.

When William McKinley entered the White House in 1897 as America's twenty-fifth president,

Ida was determined to fulfill her responsibility as first lady of the country. For receiving lines, she dressed in elegant attire, greeting visitors from a blue velvet chair. In an effort to avoid the painful activity of shaking hands, she held a large bouquet. Although attending functions was strenuous for her, Ida was present at most of the required

ABOVE: *Although Ida McKinley suffered from epileptic attacks, severe headaches, and depression, she made a substantial effort to fulfill her White House obligations.*

receptions, open houses, and dinners. However, it was the president who planned the events, making decisions about menus and decorations and giving instructions regarding serving.

During state dinners, protocol required the president to escort the wife of the guest of honor into the dining room and seat her immediately on his right. But because of his wife's condition, President McKinley dropped this practice and instead entered with his wife on his arm, seating her to his right. During dinner, if Ida had a seizure, the president would cover her face with his napkin or handkerchief and, much to the surprise of the guests, continue the conversation as if nothing unusual was happening. The only time that he was less than totally solicitous to the needs of his wife was during the Spanish-American War in 1898, when his position as president took priority.

Despite her illness, Ida enjoyed traveling. At the beginning of her husband's second term in 1901, Ida, her maid, her niece, and the White House physician joined the president on a six-week tour of the South and West. In September of that year, she joined her husband in Buffalo, New York. During that trip, after a tiring visit to Niagara Falls on September 6, Ida retired to her room to rest instead of attending a reception at the Pan-American Exposition with her husband. Only a few hours later, the president was shot. As he lay on the floor bleeding, his foremost thoughts were about his wife's health. He warned his secretary, George Cortelyou, to "be careful" in telling the first lady about the tragedy. Eight days later, President McKinley died.

Ida attended the numerous funeral ceremonies honoring the president, but she never returned to the White House. The former president's secretary sent her belongings to the McKinley home on Market Street, where she lived seizure-free until her death on May 26, 1907.

EDITH KERMIT CAROW ROOSEVELT

August 6, 1861–September 30, 1948

Theodore Roosevelt, president 1901–1909

"Mrs. Roosevelt is not only the President's wife; she is Theodore Roosevelt's

wife—vocation enough for an ordinary woman."

—Anne O'Hagan, Harper's Bazaar, May 1905

OPPOSITE: *This detail of Theobald Chartran's 1902 portrait of Edith Roosevelt shows the first lady on the South Lawn of the White House.*

While vacationing with his family in the Adirondacks, Vice President Theodore Roosevelt received word that President McKinley was dying. By the time Roosevelt reached Buffalo, the president was dead. On September 14, 1901, immediately following McKinley's death, forty-two-year-old Theodore Roosevelt was sworn in as America's twenty-sixth president. One week later, the entire Roosevelt clan, complete with six children—seventeen-year-old Alice (a daughter from Theodore's first marriage) being the oldest and four-year-old Quentin being the youngest—arrived at the White House. Suddenly, in addition to being a wife, homemaker, and mother and referee to six rowdy children, Edith Roosevelt took on the large responsibility of being the nation's first lady.

Edith Carow, the daughter of Gertrude Tyler and Charles Carow, was born in Norwich, Connecticut, in 1861. She grew up in New York City next door to Theodore Roosevelt's family, with whom she became well acquainted, as Edith and Theodore's sisters traveled in the same privileged social circles. By the time that Theodore left for Harvard in 1875, he and Edith were secretly engaged. Sometime later, the young sweethearts had a quarrel and Theodore broke off the engagement. During his junior year in college, he met wealthy Boston socialite Alice Hathaway Lee, whom he married after graduation. A few years later, on February 13, 1884, while serving as an assemblyman in the New York State legislature, Roosevelt received a telegram that prompted him to rush home because his mother and wife were seriously ill. The next day, his mother died from typhoid fever. Later that evening, his twenty-two-year-old wife died from childbirth complications and Bright's disease. Unable to cope with his overwhelming grief, Roosevelt left his infant daughter with his sister and moved to the Dakota Badlands, where for two years he immersed himself in the strenuous life of a cattle rancher. While on a visit home to New York, he happened upon his former companion Edith. They renewed their friendship and before long found that they still cared for each other. The two were married on December 2, 1886.

When the lively Roosevelt family moved into the White House, they brought with them a menagerie of pets including lizards, dogs, cats, a snake (named Emily Spinach) belonging to Alice, and a pony that had access to every bedroom in the White House. As for the children themselves, they were a rambunctious and mischievous group. Antique furnishings were used as trampolines, and spitballs were aimed at presidential portraits; if the children were not walking on stilts, they were bowling, roller-skating, or sliding down the staircase on large serving trays they found in the kitchen. Ever the pranksters, they dropped water balloons on the heads of guards and delighted in shocking visitors with Alice's pet snake.

Edith Roosevelt skillfully performed her official duties as the nation's hostess while managing to be a full-time mother. She also assisted the

president by opening his mail, clipping news articles that she thought would be of interest to him, monitoring his meals, and making him stick to a 10:30 P.M. bedtime. To help keep order, Edith hired a social secretary and press agent, making her the

RIGHT: *This popular 1903 photograph of President Theodore Roosevelt and his family gathered on the lawn at Sagamore Hill, the Roosevelt estate, appeared on many postcards during that era. From left to right are: Quentin, President Roosevelt, Theodore Jr. (the oldest son), Archibald (on his father's knee), Alice (the president's daughter from his first marriage), Kermit, Edith, and Ethel.*

OPPOSITE: *Edith Roosevelt wore this robin's egg–blue silk brocade gown at the presidential inaugural ball on March 4, 1905. The design features ostrich feathers in a swirling raised pattern. After the dress was completed, the surplus fabric was destroyed to prevent it from being reproduced. The dress as shown here has been altered since the time that Edith first wore it; the skirt is not as full and the bodice, save for the rose-point lace around the square neck, is not original.*

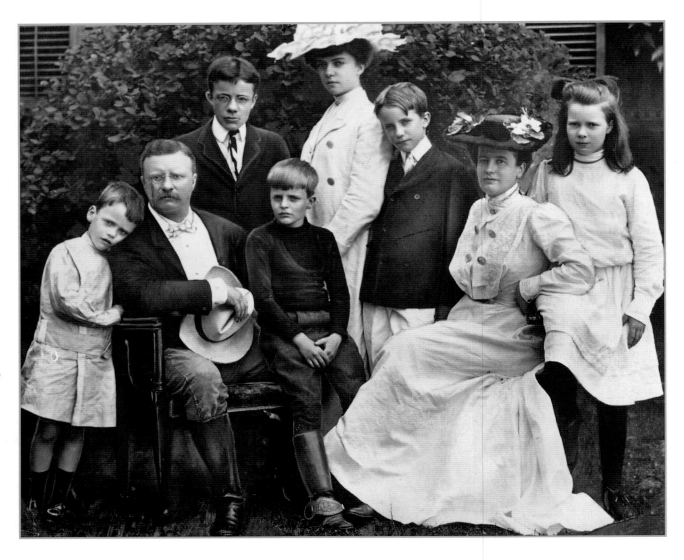

first woman in her position to do so. Nearly every day and evening, some kind of social event was scheduled for the president, the first lady, or one of the children. At their first New Year's Day open house in 1902, President and Mrs. Roosevelt greeted nine thousand visitors. Two days later, seven hundred young people, cabinet members, and relatives attended Alice's debutante party. Alice, dubbed "Princess Alice" by the press, was the darling of the American public, who enjoyed her quick wit and sharp tongue and liked reading about her adventures, romances, and parties.

During the Roosevelt administration, the White House underwent a major remodeling at a cost of $475,000. This was the single largest remodeling since the reconstruction that had followed the War of 1812. During this undertaking, the State Dining Room was enlarged and the East and West Wings were added—a measure that finally took the president's office out of the family quarters. Unfortunately, in order to make room for the new West Wing, the greenhouses had to be demolished. Also at the last public auction of White House furnishings, old items such as Tiffany screens from Chester A. Arthur's administration (1881–1885), gilded mirrors, mantels, and outdated bedroom and office fixtures went up for sale. In the newly redone downstairs corridor, Edith had portraits of the previous first ladies displayed. Like Caroline Harrison, she continued to catalog china patterns from earlier administrations and exhibit them prominently. In addition, the Roosevelts

RIGHT: *Although Edith Roosevelt preferred privacy, she recognized the public's interest in the first family. Achieving a balance between her desires and those of the nation's citizens, she worked closely with her social secretary, Belle Hagner, to control the photographs and information that would be given to the press. Here, she is photographed sitting in the White House Green Room.*

commissioned their own state service, which was regularly used.

The New Year's Day open house in 1903 gave the public its first chance to view the newly refurbished White House. As first lady, Edith Roosevelt presided over teas, state dinners, open houses, and public receptions. Nearly every Friday evening during the social season, she hosted a musicale for two hundred to five hundred guests. One of the largest social events took place on February 17, 1906, when her stepdaughter Alice married Representative Nicholas Longworth of Ohio. One thousand guests attended the East Room wedding, and presents poured in from all over the world.

The opulent wedding exceeded even the extravagant nuptials of President Grant's daughter, Nellie, which had taken place thirty-two years earlier.

After having served almost two full terms, President Theodore Roosevelt decided not to seek office again, instead encouraging his secretary of war, William Taft, to run on the Republican ticket. With the strong support of the president, Taft won the election. A little over a decade later, in 1919, Roosevelt died of a coronary embolism. Edith died in 1948 at the age of eighty-seven, having survived her husband by more than twenty-nine years. They are buried next to each other in Oyster Bay, New York.

LEFT: *After Theodore's death in 1919, Edith traveled abroad and kept Sagamore Hill as her home. She continued actively supporting the Needlework Guild, a charity that provided clothing to the poor, and remained involved with Christ Church at Oyster Bay. Although she tended to avoid public appearances, during the 1930s she campaigned on behalf of Republican presidential candidate Herbert Hoover. Here, she is shown addressing the National Conference of Republican Women.*

HELEN HERRON TAFT

June 2, 1861–May 22, 1943

William Howard Taft, president 1909–1913

"I could not feel that I was mistress of any house if I did not take an active interest in all of the details of running it."

—Helen Taft

*H*elen Herron, known as "Nellie" to her family and friends, was born in Cincinnati in 1861 to Harriet Collins and Judge John W. Herron. Her father took an active interest in politics, and at an early age Helen learned to enjoy political conversations as much as he. When she was a teenager, Helen and her family were often guests of President Hayes (a former law partner of Judge Herron) and his family at the White House. She was quite taken with the lifestyle and vowed someday to marry a man who would be president.

Helen attended Miss Nourse's School along with other girls from Cincinnati's elite families and then took classes at Miami University. Ambitious and driven, she was not content to stay at home. Although her wealthy family could easily have supported her, she began teaching. She also organized a small group of intellectual men and women into a salon, and they discussed literary topics, music, and politics. One member of her group was William Howard Taft, a recent Yale graduate who had just returned home to Cincinnati to begin a law practice. The agreeable and pleasant Will was in awe of the young, outspoken teacher who drank beer and smoked. He pursued her until she finally agreed to marry him. After a one-year engagement, the couple wed in the home of Helen's family on June 19, 1886.

The following year, Will was appointed as a judge to the Ohio Superior Court. His lifelong dream of becoming a justice of the U.S. Supreme Court now seemed possible. His wife, however, had other plans. She wanted to live in the White House and was determined that her husband become president. So Helen decided to manage his career. After the United States acquired the Philippines at the end of the Spanish-American War, President McKinley appointed Will head of a commission to establish a civil government there. Will was reluctant to accept the assignment, but Helen saw this as a golden opportunity for political advancement and insisted her husband take it.

In 1900 the Taft family, which included two sons and one daughter ranging from three to eleven years of age, moved into the elegant Malacanan Palace in the Philippines. Will Taft worked to establish postwar order and then was appointed governor-general. After the death of President McKinley, Theodore Roosevelt, who was a close friend of Taft, became president. Roosevelt knew how much Taft wanted a seat on the Supreme Court and offered one to Taft twice. Both times Helen refused to allow him to accept the much desired position, wanting him instead to wait for a chance to run for the presidency. In 1904, President Roosevelt offered Taft the position of secretary of war. Knowing a cabinet appointment could be a stepping-stone to the office of chief executive, Helen permitted her husband to take the post. In 1908, when Theodore Roosevelt decided not to seek another term, he enthusiastically endorsed Taft. The latter defeated Democrat William Jennings Bryan to become America's twenty-seventh president.

After the inauguration on March 4, 1909, outgoing President Theodore Roosevelt decided to go directly to the train station instead of taking the traditional ride back to the White House with the incoming president. When Helen saw that the seat next to her husband was available, she took advantage of the opportunity and quickly climbed into the carriage. This marked the first instance in which a first lady rode beside her husband in the inaugural parade.

Helen was elated to have realized her dream of becoming first lady. Immediately, she set about making changes in the staff, firing the steward and hiring a housekeeper to take care of the details of running such a large house. Pleased overall with the changes made in the White House during the Roosevelt administration, she made only a few alter-ations, one of which was the installation of an extra-large bathtub for her more than three-hundred-pound (136kg) husband. When Helen realized that the $12,000 transportation allotment for automobiles was not enough for more than a few serviceable cars, she struck a deal with Pierce-Arrow and the White Company. For an agreed-upon discount, she purchased a Pierce-Arrow and a White steamer; in exchange, the companies were able to advertise the fact that they supplied automobiles to the White House. The Tafts were the first White House family to use automobiles, which were housed in the stable along with the horses.

Unfortunately, only two months after becoming first lady, Helen had a stroke that left her partially paralyzed. Her husband, despite his presidential duties, rarely left her bedside, nursing her back to health and helping her learn to speak again. During this time, the couple's daughter, also named Helen, and the first lady's three sisters took over the duties of White House hostess. Receiving excellent care, Helen made a remarkable recovery and was able to resume control of the White House within the year.

As first lady, Helen was intimately involved in her husband's presidency. She was responsible for one diplomat being recalled because she felt he had slighted her twenty years earlier. When Representative Nicholas Longworth was recom-mended as minister to China, Helen convinced her husband to reject the appointment because of her personal dislike for his wife, Alice Roosevelt Longworth. Helen attended cabinet meetings and consistently invited herself into private conversa-tions between the president and other leaders. In general, she preferred participating in the political discussions of men to conversing about less weighty matters with her female guests—much like Sarah Polk more than half a century earlier.

When Tokyo mayor Yukio Ozaki sent three thousand cherry tree saplings as a gift to Helen

Taft, she had them planted near the Potomac River in an area known as the Tidal Basin. She also had a beautiful promenade built there, as well as two bandstands. Because of her efforts, this formerly muddy area was transformed into a place for the fashionable Washington set to be seen. Unfortunately, the trees were infected and had to be burned. When the mayor of Tokyo found out that the trees needed to be destroyed, he sent three thousand more that were successfully planted. This beautification act was the beginning of the annual Cherry Blossom Festival that still brings thousands of tourists to Washington each year.

The Tafts enjoyed entertaining, and rarely a day went by without a function. Helen held three "at homes" weekly. She hosted state dinners, congressional dinners, breakfasts, luncheons, musicales, garden parties for two thousand people, and small, intimate get-togethers just for friends. Two of the largest receptions included a debutante party for the Tafts' daughter in 1909 and the couple's silver wedding anniversary in 1911.

Both Will and Helen Taft were disappointed to leave the White House when Woodrow Wilson won the 1912 presidential election. Helen was so upset about departing that she didn't bother to say goodbye to the White House staff. The former president accepted a professorship at Yale University, where he taught law. In 1921, his lifelong dream finally came true when President Warren Harding appointed him chief justice of the Supreme Court. Happy to return to Washington, Helen did not object to her husband's appointment this time. She died shortly before her eighty-second birthday, having survived her husband by thirteen years. The couple are buried next to each other in Arlington National Cemetery.

ELLEN LOUISE AXSON WILSON

May 15, 1860–August 6, 1914
Woodrow Wilson, president 1913–1921

"I wonder how anyone who reaches middle age can bear it if she cannot feel, on looking back, that whatever mistakes she may have made she has on the whole lived for others and not for herself."

—Ellen Wilson

OPPOSITE: *Ellen (pictured) and Woodrow Wilson were prolific letter writers throughout their thirty-year marriage. In one of her last letters to her husband, Ellen wrote, "My life has been the most remarkable life history that I ever even read about—and to think I have lived it with you! I love you, my dear, in every way you could wish to be loved. Deeply, tenderly, devotedly, passionately."*

Ellen Louise Axson was born in Savannah, Georgia, to Margaret Hoyt and the Reverend Samuel E. Axson, the latter a Presbyterian minister. In 1883, twenty-three-year-old Ellen met Woodrow Wilson, a young Atlanta lawyer and son of a Presbyterian minister, during a visit by him to her father's church in Rome, Georgia. Woodrow was immediately infatuated with Ellen and initiated a courtship that lasted about two years. Although they were in different places during that time— she in New York City attending the Art Student's League and he in Baltimore at Johns Hopkins University finishing his graduate work—they wrote to each other almost daily. On June 24, 1885, the couple married. Woodrow's career, which took them to a number of different places, included teaching at universities, writing books, acting as president of Princeton University, and serving as governor of New Jersey. In 1912, he was elected president of the United States.

In March 1913, Ellen and Woodrow Wilson quietly moved into the White House with their three daughters, ages twenty, twenty-two, and twenty-three. The Wilsons were not known for lively entertainment. Even the inaugural ball was cancelled because they believed it to be frivolous. Dutifully, Ellen presided over semiweekly receptions and the occasional state dinner, always with unassuming dignity. The family much preferred small dinners with their friends to large, obligatory social functions.

When Ellen entered the White House, she was determined to make her tenure as first lady meaningful. She became involved in various service projects, such as having rest rooms installed for female government workers. She also sold many of her paintings to support various charities. As an artist, she appreciated the work of a group of women in Appalachia who made textiles and various other handicrafts. In fact, she was so impressed by these women that she became a strong supporter of an association that aided and educated them. What's more, she gave these talented women much publicity by purchasing baskets and rugs for the White House, as well as textiles for covering furniture and making draperies.

As a member of the board of Associated Charities in Washington, Ellen was involved in many public service activities. She was appalled when she learned of the filthy living conditions to which many immigrants and poor people in the nation's capital were subject. In a desperate attempt to help these impoverished citizens, she lobbied Congress for assistance. Ellen believed that if the slums were cleared and made into parks, not only would the city look better, but the poor would be able to find decent housing. Ultimately, Congress did pass a slum clearance bill known as the "Alley Bill" or "Mrs. Wilson's Bill," which cleared out much of these areas. Though the legislation created parks

and small streets where the slums previously existed, no provision was made for relocating those who had been living in the cleared areas. Because the displaced people had nowhere to go, the bill simply resulted in creating additional slums instead of beautifying the city and improving the quality of life for those Ellen had intended to help.

Granted, Ellen Wilson preferred her work as an activist to planning social functions or refurbishing the old mansion. Nonetheless, she did undertake a modest amount of redecorating in the private bed-rooms. And it was the grounds of the White House on which Ellen really made her mark, filling a small, undistinguished plot of land near the West Wing with roses and carved limestone furniture. This charming setting, in which President and Mrs. Wilson spent many happy hours, aptly became known as the Rose Garden and continues to be a source of enjoyment for residents and visitors alike.

During Edith and Woodrow Wilson's time together in the White House, two of their daughters,

OPPOSITE: *Ellen Wilson was a gifted artist. Although determining the subject of her painting* The Terrace *(circa 1913) has involved much debate, it is now thought to be the terrace at Prospect House—the residence of the president of Princeton University. Woodrow Wilson held that position from 1902 to 1910.*

LEFT: *Posing outside the White House are, from left to right, Ellen Wilson and daughters Eleanor, Margaret, and Jessie. Jessie and Eleanor both had White House weddings during their father's first term. Margaret was a talented soprano, who entertained army troops during World War I.*

Jessie and Eleanor, got married. In November 1913, Jessie wed attorney Frank Sayre in an elaborate East Room ceremony. Six months later, Eleanor married William G. McAdoo, the secretary of the treasury. The later wedding was more subdued and took place in the Blue Room because Ellen, who had become ill with Bright's disease, was too weak to plan another large event. In August 1914, three months after the McAdoos exchanged their vows, Ellen lost her battle with the illness. She is buried next to her parents in Rome, Georgia. Despite her short seventeen months as first lady, Ellen Wilson accomplished a great deal and left a long-lasting legacy.

EDITH BOLLING GALT WILSON

October 15, 1872–December 28, 1961
Woodrow Wilson, president 1913–1921

"I followed day by day every phase of the mosaic which he was shaping into a pattern of statecraft, and we continued this partnership of thought and comradeship unbroken to the last day of his life."

—Edith Wilson

OPPOSITE: *Edith Wilson became first lady when she married President Woodrow Wilson on December 18, 1915. On the way to their honeymoon destination, the happy groom danced in their private railcar, singing to his bride, "Oh, you beautiful doll. You great big beautiful doll." This portrait of Edith was painted by Emile Alexay in 1924.*

Edith Bolling, born in Wytheville, Virginia, in 1872, was the daughter of Sallie White and Judge William Bolling. She was also a seventh-generation descendant of Pocahontas. Although Edith's father had been a wealthy plantation owner, he was left nearly destitute after the Civil War. She received a basic education from her paternal grandmother, who taught her reading, writing, music, and poetry. When Edith was eighteen, she accepted an invitation from her oldest sister for an extended visit to Washington. While there, Edith met Norman Galt, a jeweler. They married in 1896.

Being the wife of a wealthy businessman opened doors for Edith. The couple took annual tours of Europe and attended parties hosted by Washington's most influential men and women. After her husband's death in 1908, Edith was left with financial security and an assured place in Washington society.

The White House was still in official mourning when grief-stricken President Wilson met Edith Galt six months after Ellen Wilson's death. The president's cousin Helen Bones introduced the two. From the moment they met, the charming, intelligent Mrs. Galt captivated the newly widowed president. Their courtship included rides in the country, walks, and sailing excursions. The president also had a private telephone line installed between the White House and Edith's home, openly discussing affairs of state with her. Only two months after their first meeting, Wilson proposed. Edith turned him down, as it had been less than a year since the death of his wife. Moreover, she found the idea of being married to the president of the United States overwhelming. When Edith did finally accept, the press had a field day; the announcement of the president's upcoming nuptials was considered such big news that it bumped information regarding the war in Europe from the headlines.

Not everyone was pleased with the president's marriage plans. His three daughters felt he was betraying their mother's memory, and his political advisors worried that remarrying too soon after Ellen's death might compromise his chances for reelection. The person who most objected was Wilson's personal friend and political advisor Colonel Edward House, who tried to stop the marriage. He resented Edith's closeness to the president, and she in turn resented his relationship with Wilson. Although they acted cordially to each other, the battle between Colonel House and Edith lasted for the duration of President Wilson's administration.

Despite the various objections, Woodrow Wilson and Edith Bolling Galt were married on December 18, 1915, making Wilson the third president to marry while in office. The wedding took place in the parlor of Edith's Washington home, which brimmed with ferns, roses, and orchids for the occasion. Filling the setting with music, a small orchestra from the Marine Corps Band played for the fifty guests. After the ceremony, the couple

boarded a train for their honeymoon in Hot Springs, Virginia. As expected, wedding gifts poured in from all over the world. Manufacturers sent samples of their merchandise, and American housewives sent their handiwork. Rugs, a Ming bowl, clocks, jewelry, crystal, linens, and all kinds of food were received.

Edith stepped into the role of first lady by hosting a reception in January 1916. With an appropriation from Congress, she purchased a

RIGHT: *Worn by Edith Wilson, this gown is made primarily of white satin embellished with silver thread. The flowing, diaphanous "angel-wing" sleeves are made of tulle. This material also appears in the bodice, which is embellished with pearls.*

1,700-piece china service. Designed by Lenox China, this was the first American-made service ever acquired for the White House. Entertaining was suspended, however, when the United States entered World War I in April 1917, and the White House gates were closed.

Even though very little formal entertaining was taking place (there were some luncheons and dinners for foreign diplomats), Edith stayed extremely busy during this period by making contributions to the war effort. So that she could assist her country, she was taught how to decode and encode military and diplomatic messages coming into and leaving the White House. In order to save manpower, Edith allowed sheep to graze on the White House lawn, thereby keeping the grass trimmed. The presence of the sheep brought the bonus of a supply of wool, which was auctioned off to raise $100,000 for the war effort. Edith also honored the rationing laws, such as gasless Sundays, meatless Mondays, and wheatless Tuesdays, using her position to set an example for women across the country. Last but not least, she donned a uniform and volunteered at the Red Cross canteen in Washington. At the conclusion of World War I, Edith accompanied the president to Paris for the signing of the peace accord. While he was in sessions working on the agreement, she visited hospitals, factories, and rehabilitation centers.

In the summer of 1919, the president traveled across the United States, trying to get support for his League of Nations, designed to uphold international peace. In September of that year, he suffered a stroke that left him a semiparalyzed invalid. The doctors advised Edith to shield the president from any stress. Feeling that it was her job to protect both her husband's position and health, Edith began what she referred to as her "stewardship" of the presidency. It was she who made the decisions regarding who would visit the president, and it was

she who determined which papers were necessary for him to see. Since the president had difficulty reading and writing because of the stroke, she would read vital documents, summarize the contents for him, and then return the papers to officials with her initials.

The only people allowed to see the president were his wife, his private secretary—Joseph P. Tumulty—and his doctors. Not even Vice President Thomas Marshall or cabinet members were permitted to see Wilson after his stroke. Edith received

ABOVE: *At the end of World War I, Edith Wilson accompanied her husband to Europe for the Paris Peace Conference. Because of his contributions to this process, President Wilson was awarded the Nobel Peace Prize in 1920.*

RIGHT: *After Woodrow Wilson's stroke, Edith began what she referred to as her "stewardship" of the presidency. Although Edith clearly exercised tremendous power, she was opposed to women having the right to vote and was critical of the suffragists who picketed outside the gates of the White House.*

OPPOSITE, TOP: *Edith Wilson is shown in this photograph (far right) during a visit to the Kennedy White House in November 1961, a month before her death at the age of eighty-nine.*

OPPOSITE, BOTTOM: *The state service ordered by Edith Wilson was the first to be made in the United States. Produced by Lenox China in Trenton, New Jersey, the service was also the first to bear the presidential seal.*

massive criticism for her role in allegedly running the country during this time. Wilson's political enemies referred to this period of his administration as a "petticoat government." It was not until April 1920 that Wilson held another cabinet meeting.

After the inauguration of Warren G. Harding in 1921, the Wilsons retired to a luxurious town house on Washington's S Street, purchased for them by their wealthy friends. Woodrow Wilson died there three years later at the age of sixty-seven. He is buried at the National Cathedral, making him the only president to be buried in Washington. For the next thirty-seven years, Mrs. Wilson remained a highly respected figure in Washington society. In one of her last public appearances, she was a guest of President Kennedy at his inauguration in January 1961. The former first lady died on December 28, 1961, her husband's birthday. She is buried next to him at the National Cathedral.

FLORENCE KLING HARDING

August 15, 1860–November 21, 1924
Warren G. Harding, president 1921–1923

"Well, Warren Harding, I have got you the Presidency;

what are you going to do with it?"

—*Florence Harding*

A native of Marion, Ohio, Florence Kling was born in 1860 to Louisa Bouton and Amos Kling. Her father, a prominent banker, wanted another son and was unhappy when he learned that his third child was a girl. Making his disappointment no secret, Kling raised Florence as if she were a boy and the young girl grew up knowing that she was unwanted by her harsh disciplinarian father.

A gifted musician, Florence attended the Cincinnati Conservatory of Music. At the age of nineteen, she eloped with her next-door neighbor, Henry DeWolfe, and six months later she gave birth

to a son, Marshall. Her husband, an abusive alcoholic who couldn't hold on to a job, abandoned Florence and the baby, leaving her destitute and homeless. In 1884, Florence divorced her husband and moved back to Marion, hoping that her father would forgive her for the elopement and take her in. He agreed to let her live with him, but only if she would take back her maiden name and give custody of her son to him. At first Florence refused, supporting herself and her son with money she earned giving piano lessons and some assistance from her former in-laws. But when Marshall was four years old, Florence acquiesced and gave custody

RIGHT: *Florence Harding wore this evening gown and wrap during her tenure as first lady. Both pieces incorporate sequins and rhinestones to yield a shimmering effect. Although Mrs. Harding wore the garments together, they were created by two different dressmakers.*

to her father. She then severed her relationship with
her son as well as the rest of her family.

In 1890, Florence met Warren Harding, the
owner of the local weekly newspaper, the *Marion
Star*. Warren was pursued by the aggressive and
strong-willed Florence for two years before he
agreed to marriage. The thirty-year-old Florence
and twenty-five-year-old Warren were married on
July 8, 1891.

Florence began pitching in at the *Star* and
helped to build the small, struggling newspaper
into a successful daily publication. She encouraged
Warren to run for office and became the driving
force behind his political career. When he campaigned for the U.S. Senate after having held other
political offices, she organized his schedule and
became the campaign treasurer.

In 1920, when Warren Harding ran for president, Florence was acutely aware of the emerging
political influence of women voters. To homemakers, she appeared as a devoted and supportive wife.
To others, she was a progressive feminist business
woman. Florence's own experience with and
understanding of the media, combined with her
knack for making the most of photo opportunities,
served her husband well in the first national election in which women had the right to vote. In
1921, Warren Harding was sworn in as America's
twenty-ninth president.

As first lady, Florence welcomed the throngs of
people anxious to get a glimpse inside the White
House. During World War I and President Wilson's
illness, the Executive Mansion had been a locked
fortress. Now the gates were once again open and

ABOVE: *Florence Harding
stands in line in front of her
husband, waiting to cast her
ballot in 1920. This was the
first presidential election in
which women had the right
to vote.*

123

RIGHT: *Florence hosts the wives of Philippine delegates seeking independence for the archipelago.*

sightseers were welcomed. Florence even opened the shades and waved at people looking inside, acknowledging that it was the people's White House. She would often interact with those taking White House tours, pointing out objects of interest.

The Hardings entertained regularly, often hosting garden parties for thousands of people. They especially enjoyed entertaining veterans from area hospitals. Delighting in public events, the first lady generously supported many charitable causes with her presence. Although she liked the limelight, Florence was sensitive about her looks, particularly her sagging, aging skin. Often, she wore a wide black velvet collar to hide her neck. She also called in a skin specialist to the White House for daily facials.

While Florence Harding was cheerful and hospitable in public, behind closed doors she was jealous and vindictive. When the widow of Senator John Henderson offered to give her mansion on Sixteenth Street to the U.S. government to be used as a permanent residence for the vice president, Mrs. Harding wouldn't stand for it. She immediately went into action, telling everyone with any influence to vote against the bill that would have accepted the house. When the bill was indeed defeated, she jubilantly announced, "I just couldn't have people like those Coolidges living in that beautiful house."

Florence also kept what she referred to as a "grudge book," which she had started back when

from Ohio, be named chief of the Veterans Administration. The choice was a poor one, to say the least, as Forbes was eventually convicted of stealing millions of dollars appropriated for injured veterans. One of the most famous scandals involved the Teapot Dome Oil Reserve in Wyoming, which Secretary of the Interior Albert Fall had convinced President Harding to sign over to his department; Fall then sold oil rights for hundreds of thousands of dollars. To top it all off, during this time of prohibition in America, liquor was banned from the Executive Mansion, but when the Treasury Department confiscated the best gin, it was relocated to 1600 Pennsylvania Avenue, where the first lady, called "Duchess" by her husband and their friends, acted as bartender.

By June 1923, public criticism of Harding's corruption-filled administration was leading to an investigation. But the president suddenly became ill while on vacation in the West and died in San Francisco on June 20, 1923. When Florence refused to allow an autopsy, speculation about the cause of death ran from food poisoning to murder. During the weeks following the president's death, Florence meticulously went through her husband's papers and burned anything that she felt might be incriminating. She died seventeen months later at the age of sixty-four and is buried next to her husband in her hometown of Marion.

LEFT: *The first lady signs autographs for Girl Scouts visiting the White House in 1922. Resting at Florence's feet is the president's popular Airedale terrier, Laddie Boy.*

her husband became a U.S. senator. In this book, she wrote the names of her enemies and vowed revenge. Among these names were two of her husband's mistresses—Carrie Phillips, who was the wife of his best friend, and Nan Britton, who two years before Harding's election had allegedly given birth to his daughter.

But the Hardings had bigger problems on their hands than Florence's personal battles, for the administration was filled with corruption and scandal. As president, Warren Harding was not a strong leader and he depended on others, including his wife, for advice. He consulted Florence on federal appointments, and it was Florence who insisted that Charles Forbes, one of their associates

GRACE ANNA GOODHUE COOLIDGE

January 3, 1879–July 8, 1957
Calvin Coolidge, president 1923–1929

"It is too bad that more women cannot have the opportunity of living in the White House. It is a great opportunity for service."

—*Grace Coolidge*

Grace Anna Goodhue, daughter of Lemira Barrett and Andrew Goodhue, was born in Burlington, Vermont, where she grew up in a comfortable middle-class environment. After graduating from the University of Vermont in 1902, she joined the teaching staff at the Clarke School for the Deaf in Northampton, Massachusetts. In 1903, Grace met Calvin Coolidge, a local lawyer and the Hampshire County clerk of courts. They were immediately attracted to each other and started a courtship that lasted two years, culminating in their wedding on October 4, 1905, at her parents' home in Burlington.

Grace and Calvin were an unlikely pair. Where Calvin was sober, frugal, reserved, and obsessed with holding office, Grace was outgoing and friendly with very little interest in politics. Although she never got involved with her husband's political career, she was proud of his accomplishments. Calvin served in numerous elected positions, from mayor of Northampton to governor of Massachusetts. In 1920, when he became vice president under Warren Harding, he was thrust onto the national stage. Grace enjoyed living in Washington, where she became an admired member of the social set.

The Coolidges were visiting Calvin's father at his Plymouth, New Hampshire, farm when word came that President Harding had died. Coolidge's father, in his capacity as notary public and justice of the peace, administered the oath of office to his son, swearing Calvin in as the new president at 2:47 A.M. on August 3, 1923. The family then went back to bed.

As first lady, Grace enjoyed being in the public arena. She gladly stood in receiving lines, rode in parades, presided over luncheons and dinners, volunteered for the Red Cross, and attended tree plantings and ribbon-cutting ceremonies. She donated a great deal of her time to fund-raisers that benefited deaf children. Like many of her predecessors, Grace recognized the value attached to the position of first lady and used that power to promote women's organizations.

Among the many people who stayed at the White House as guests of the Coolidges were the Prince of Wales, the queen of Romania, aviator Charles Lindbergh, entertainer and humorist Will Rogers, and movie stars Mary Pickford and Douglas Fairbanks. Grace hosted twice-weekly teas, musicales, and frequent dinners. The president's seriousness and reluctance to waste words

ABOVE: *When it came to her husband's political actions, Grace Coolidge knew only what she read in the papers. Unlike many presidents, Calvin Coolidge did not discuss such matters with his wife. She only learned of her husband's decision not to run for reelection in 1928 when reporters approached her for comment.*

RIGHT: *This red chiffon velvet flapper-style evening dress with a rhinestone belt was worn by Grace Coolidge during her husband's administration. The dress also has a detachable train and coordinating velvet shoes.*

OPPOSITE, TOP: *Grace Coolidge actively worked on behalf of a number of charitable causes. In addition to heading the national honorary committees of the Red Cross and the American Legion Endowment Fund, she often donned a Red Cross uniform and visited disabled veterans at the Walter Reed Army Hospital in Washington.*

earned him the nickname "Silent Cal." At dinners, Grace often filled in the president's long periods of silence with humorous comments, making everyone feel comfortable.

The Coolidges' style was reserved and dignified. Even when the family was dining alone, everyone dressed for dinner. Although President Coolidge had a reputation for being a penny-pincher, there was one area in which he spent freely: his wife's wardrobe. He thoroughly enjoyed buying her expensive clothes and hats and insisted that her ensembles be of top quality. He was accustomed to being in charge and could be somewhat authoritarian toward his wife. However, Grace was capable of demonstrating a mind of her own. Once, when her husband forbade her to speak to reporters, she answered their questions in sign language.

On January 1, 1924, the Coolidges resumed the traditional New Year's Day open house, which had been suspended during the war years. More than three thousand people came through the White House that day. In the summer of that year, Calvin Jr., the younger of the Coolidges' two sons, developed a blister after playing tennis on the White House lawn. The wound became infected, and he suffered from blood poisoning. Sadly, he died four days later, at only sixteen years of age. The White House went into mourning and much of the enjoyment that the Coolidges felt while living in the White House was lost. Even though the president refused to campaign during that election year, he easily defeated his opponent. Since the first family was still in mourning, the inaugural ceremony was somber. The inaugural ball was replaced with an afternoon reception for state governors and a small family party in the evening.

In 1927, the White House underwent some remodeling. The roof was replaced and a new third floor, which included a bright sunroom with windows on three sides, was added. Mrs. Coolidge

BELOW: *While she was first lady, Grace Coolidge crocheted this coverlet for the Lincoln bed. She incorporated the dates of her husband's administration and her name into the design. The textile remains in the White House.*

called this comfortable new living area her "sky room." On the main floor, the Green Room, which had been used extensively, was badly in need of an update. With the help of an advisory committee, the first lady furnished the room with quality Federal pieces. Before leaving the White House, she crocheted a coverlet for the Lincoln bed. The design incorporated an eagle, the Liberty Bell, and other patriotic themes. There was so much public interest in the bedcover that instructions for making it were printed in several large city newspapers.

After leaving the White House in 1929, the Coolidges retired to Northampton, Massachusetts. The former president died almost four years later. Grace lived for another twenty-four years. She became a trustee of the Clarke School for the Deaf and continued to support many charitable causes. She died at the age of seventy-eight and is buried beside her husband in Plymouth, New Hampshire.

LOU HENRY HOOVER

March 29, 1874–January 7, 1944
Herbert Hoover, president 1929–1933

"It is perfectly possible to have both a home and a career. In this modern age we are released from so many of the burdens our grandmothers and great-grandmothers had to bear."

—Lou Hoover

Lou Henry, daughter of Florence Weed and banker Charles D. Henry, was born in Waterloo, Iowa, in 1874. She grew up enjoying basketball, archery, skating, hunting, fishing, and camping. While attending Stanford University, she met fellow geology student Herbert Hoover. After she earned a degree in geology in 1898, Lou married Herbert on February 10, 1899, in her parents' home. The newlyweds immediately left for China, where Herbert had obtained a job as chief engineer for the Chinese Engineering and Mining Company. Already fluent in four languages, Lou quickly mastered Chinese and was able to help her husband translate materials and give instructions to workers.

The Hoovers' two sons, born in 1903 and 1907, traveled with them to different mining assignments all over the world. At the outbreak of World War I, the family was living in London, where Herbert had started his own engineering firm. Fearing for the safety of their sons, the couple sent both boys back to America. During the war, both Lou and Herbert became active in relief efforts, such as aiding American travelers who were stranded in Europe and distributing food and supplies. Through these actions, Herbert earned a reputation for being an outstanding administrator. In 1921, President Harding appointed Herbert secretary of commerce, a post he continued to hold under Coolidge's administration. When Coolidge declined to run for reelection in 1928, Herbert Hoover easily won the presidency.

As first lady, Mrs. Hoover endorsed many women's causes, including the Girl Scouts, the League of Women Voters, the Campfire Girls, and the General Federation of Woman's Clubs. She also felt that the White House should give the visiting public a sense of the past. Toward that end, she researched the history of the White House and brought out of storage many items from previous administrations for display, such as presidential portraits and historical objects. Using her own funds, Mrs. Hoover had virtually every object in the mansion documented and photographed for a permanent inventory of White House furnishings.

In 1930, the Hoovers stood in line and shook hands with many of the more than six thousand people who had come to the traditional New Year's Day open house. After four hours, the exhausted president left the receiving line, even though more people were still waiting to meet him and the first lady. In late 1932, word went out that the president would no longer be at home on New Year's Day, thus bringing the tradition of the open house to an end.

The Hoovers entertained in an extravagant style, insisting on the best of everything. If the cost of a function overran the amount allowed by Congress, the wealthy president wrote a personal check to cover the difference. With their constant hosting of events, the Hoovers kept the White House staff extremely busy. Often the number of people invited to lunch or dinner would suddenly

double. Sometimes with only an hour's notice the White House kitchen staff would be forced to prepare food for hundreds of guests.

The Hoovers rarely spoke to or looked at anyone on the White House staff. To avoid speaking to a servant, Lou developed a series of hand signals indicating when it was time to serve or pick up plates. Staff members were not permitted to use the elevator or be seen by the Hoovers. When a staff member became aware that either the president or

ABOVE: *Lou Hoover lent her support to many organizations. By sending White House laundry to the Sunlight Laundry— part of the Nannie Helen Burroughs School, a residential school for black women— instead of to a commercial operation, she helped the institution to remain open during the Depression.*

RIGHT: *This circa 1895 photo-graph shows a young Lou Henry at Stanford University. Lou, who received her degree in 1898, was the first woman to major in geology at the prestigious institution.*

"belt-tightening." Although she disliked making speeches in public, she willingly spoke on the radio. As the first of the nation's first ladies to be nationally broadcast, Lou Hoover encouraged women to donate food and clothing to needy people and gave advice to help children cope with the Depression.

In order to get away from Washington for a much needed rest, the Hoovers built a private retreat in Virginia's Blue Ridge Mountains. They named it Rapidan Camp because of its location near the Rapidan River. The retreat consisted of several cabins and walking paths. It was at this site that they were able to relax and entertain infor-mally. When Mrs. Hoover discovered that there was no school for the children who lived in the area, the Hoovers had one built and hired a teacher at their own expense. After leaving office, the Hoovers donated Rapidan Camp to the govern-ment as part of the Shenandoah National Park.

In the 1932 election, President Hoover was defeated by Franklin D. Roosevelt. Before the inauguration, Mrs. Hoover invited Eleanor Roosevelt to the White House for a tour. When Mrs. Roosevelt asked to see the cooking facilities, Lou responded, "The housekeeper will have to show you the kitchens. I never go into the kitchens."

After leaving the White House, the Hoovers settled in northern California, near the Stanford campus. At the outbreak of World War II, they once again became involved in relief efforts in Europe. During the war, the Waldorf-Astoria Hotel in New York became their headquarters and second home. It was in their room at the famous hotel that the former first lady died sud-denly of a heart attack in January 1944 at the age of sixty-nine. Her husband lived another twenty years. They are buried next to each other in West Branch, Iowa.

first lady was nearby, the employee would often hide in a closet to avoid being seen. More than once a White House worker jumped into a closet already occupied by someone else.

A political storm arose when Mrs. Hoover invited Mrs. Oscar DePriest, the wife of a black congressman, to a tea for congressional wives at the White House. The incident made national news because southern Democratic members of Congress threatened a social boycott of the White House. Mrs. Hoover made no apologies and ignored the protest. Eventually, the incident was forgotten.

When the stock market crashed in 1929 and the economy plunged into a depression, the Hoovers cut back on their lavish style of entertaining. Mrs. Hoover appeared in public in cotton dresses and made speeches encouraging

LEFT, TOP: *Lou Hoover urged her young radio listeners to pitch in at home, encouraging boys as well as girls to assist in washing the dishes and general housekeeping. In this 1931 photograph, she speaks with some Girl Scouts moments before her live NBC broadcast.*

LEFT, BOTTOM: *President and Mrs. Hoover relax at Rapidan Camp—their mountain retreat. In 1928, Hoover had dispatched an aide to find a getaway that met three requirements: it needed to be within 100 miles (160.9km) of the nation's capital, have a good fishing stream, and be 2,500 feet (762m) above sea level to avoid annoying mosquitoes. The site selected was located in Virginia's Blue Ridge Mountains.*

ANNA ELEANOR ROOSEVELT

October 11, 1884–November 7, 1962

Franklin D. Roosevelt, president 1933–1945

"I marveled at her hardihood, both physical and mental. She walked for miles,

and she saw patients who were grievously and gruesomely wounded.

But I marveled most at their expressions as she leaned over them.

It was a sight I will never forget."

—*Admiral William F. Halsey on Eleanor Roosevelt's visit to Guadalcanal*

OPPOSITE: *As first lady, Eleanor Roosevelt became an advocate for labor unions promoting higher wages and better working conditions. During the Depression, she focused attention on the unemployed by working at soup kitchens.*

$\mathcal{E}$leanor Roosevelt was asked in an interview late in her life if she had any regrets regarding her time as first lady. Mrs. Roosevelt replied that she had two: that she had been unable to stop the internment of Japanese Americans during World War II and that she had not been able to get more Jewish immigrants into the country before the war.

Anna Eleanor Roosevelt, the only daughter of Anna Livingston Hall and Elliott Roosevelt (brother of Theodore Roosevelt), was born into affluence in New York City on October 11, 1884. Her mother, who was known for her beauty, was so disappointed that Eleanor was plain-looking that she called the young girl "Granny." When Eleanor was only eight years old, her mother died, at which point Eleanor and her two brothers moved in with their wealthy maternal grandmother, Mary Hall. Their father died two years later. Although Eleanor had all the luxuries she could want, she lacked affection from her cold, authoritarian grandmother. Mary hired private tutors so that Eleanor could be educated at home and refused to let the girl have much contact with children her own age. At fifteen, Eleanor was sent to Allenswood, a finishing school near London. There, the teenager developed poise and confidence. At eighteen, Eleanor returned to New York for her debut. She then became a social worker in the New York slums.

Although Eleanor did not like socializing and felt that she was a poor dancer, she dutifully attended cotillions. It was at one of these events that she happened upon Harvard student Franklin Delano Roosevelt, her fifth cousin. Each enjoyed the companionship of the other immensely. Once, Roosevelt even accompanied her to a settlement house, where he observed the deplorable conditions in which people lived.

Eleanor was surprised when the dashing, outgoing Franklin Roosevelt proposed marriage. The engagement greatly disappointed Franklin's widowed mother, the formidable Sara Delano Roosevelt, who felt that they were both too young. Despite this objection, Eleanor and Franklin were married on March 17, 1905, in New York City. The bride's uncle, President Theodore Roosevelt, gave her away.

After their honeymoon, Franklin and Eleanor settled in New York City, where they moved into a mansion—a wedding present from Sara, who not only furnished it but also hired the servants who would take care of it. Eleanor's domineering mother-in-law virtually ran the household. Eleanor was afraid that speaking out against her mother-in-law would cause a rift to develop between herself and Franklin, so she allowed Sara to make all decisions—including those regarding their young children. Eleanor even quit her job

at the settlement house because Sara feared that Eleanor would bring home germs and infect the children.

In 1911, when Franklin became a member of the state senate in Albany, Eleanor was finally able to break away from her mother-in-law. Two years later, the Roosevelts moved to Washington so that Franklin could carry out his appointment of assistant secretary of the navy. Eleanor enjoyed discussing politics and current issues. She led a happy life in the nation's capital until 1918, when she found out that her husband was involved with Lucy Mercer, a woman who had served as her own social secretary. Devastated by the betrayal of her husband, Eleanor offered to give him a divorce. Frankin, knowing that a divorce could mean the

end of his political career, agreed never to see Lucy again. Eventually, Eleanor forgave him.

In August 1921, Franklin Roosevelt contracted polio. After a painful three years of intense therapy—and with the help of his wife—he was able to walk with the aid of crutches and leg braces. Franklin was elected governor of New York in 1928, and four years later, he won the vote for president of the United States.

Eleanor wasted no time getting started in her role as first lady. She urged Congress to clean up slums, worked for equal pay for women, lobbied for child labor laws, and attended meetings on behalf of her husband. During her first year in the White House, she traveled a total of thirty-eight thousand miles (61,142km) by bus, automobile,

RIGHT: *This family photograph includes four of Eleanor and Franklin's five children (son Elliott is absent), all of whom were grown by the time the couple entered the White House. Seated in front, from left to right, are Franklin, Eleanor (holding her grandchild Anna), Anna Roosevelt Dall (holding her son Curtis Jr.), and the formidable Sara Delano Roosevelt. Standing in back, from left to right, are three of Eleanor and Franklin's sons— Franklin Jr., James, and John— and Curtis Dall, husband of Anna Roosevelt.*

LEFT: *Eleanor Roosevelt wore this lavender day dress, made of a lightweight velvet, at her husband's first inaugural ceremony. Although the garment looks like a two-piece suit, it is actually a one-piece slip-on. The unusual design is cut on the bias, giving the dress a soft drape.*

RIGHT: *Eleanor Roosevelt attends the United Nations Human Rights Commission meeting in Geneva in 1947.*

train, and airplane. In her second year, she traveled forty-two thousand miles (67,578km).

The first lady gave the president extremely detailed accounts regarding the living and working conditions she witnessed during her travels. She inspected coal mines, hospitals, slums, prisons, and many of her husband's New Deal projects. Beginning in 1935, she wrote a daily newspaper column called "My Day," in which she chronicled her activities as first lady and gave her opinions on social issues and world events. Eleanor broadcast a regular Sunday night radio program and spent much time on the lecture circuit. She insisted that she be paid for her work and then donated her wages to charities. Always an advocate for social causes, Mrs. Roosevelt resigned her membership in the Daughters of the American Revolution in

1939 when the organization refused to allow the famous black singer Marian Anderson to perform in Constitution Hall.

The first lady not only worked tirelessly for the oppressed and the poor but spent a great deal of time presiding over social functions at the White House. Among the most noteworthy visits were those of King George VI and Queen Elizabeth, Winston Churchill, and Madame Chiang Kai-shek, who came with an entourage of forty people.

At the outbreak of World War II, Eleanor Roosevelt was appointed deputy director of the Office of Civilian Defense. She worked for the fair treatment of black people in the armed forces, petitioned the State Department to allow more refugees into America, and visited the Japanese American internment camps. She traveled to the

LEFT: *In the 1960s, Eleanor Roosevelt chaired President Kennedy's Commission on the Status of Women. Here, she stands next to the president in 1962.*

South Pacific, Great Britain, and Central America, where she visited more than 400,000 American soldiers, chatting with them, signing autographs, and even relaying messages to their families back home.

The president and first lady did little entertaining during the war. Along with the rest of the country, the White House endured food rationing. When Eleanor was in town, she held teas for wounded servicemen. If she saw a soldier while she was out for a walk, she often invited him back to the White House. Many an astonished soldier found himself having lunch with the first lady at 1600 Pennsylvania Avenue.

On April 12, 1945, President Roosevelt died of a cerebral hemorrhage in Warm Springs, Georgia. Eleanor felt deeply betrayed when she discovered that Lucy Mercer had been with him when he died.

Even after her time in the White House was over, Eleanor Roosevelt continued to be a strong political force. When Harry Truman took over the presidency, he appointed Eleanor to the United States Delegation to the United Nations General Assembly. As such, she helped shape the Universal Declaration of Human Rights, which was adopted in 1948. In 1961, President John Kennedy appointed her chairperson of his Commission on the Status of Women.

The former first lady died of a blood disease on November 7, 1962, at the age of seventy-eight. During her funeral, Adlai Stevenson, U.N. ambassador and former governor of Illinois, said, "She would rather light a candle than curse the darkness. And her glow has warmed the world." Eleanor is buried next to her husband at their estate in Hyde Park, New York.

ELIZABETH VIRGINIA WALLACE TRUMAN

February 13, 1885–October 18, 1982

Harry S. Truman, president 1945–1953

"You don't need to know me."

—Bess Truman to a group of women correspondents

After offering his condolences to Eleanor Roosevelt on the evening of April 12, 1945, Harry Truman asked, "Is there anything I can do for you?" Mrs. Roosevelt replied, "Is there anything we can do for you? For you are the one in trouble now." At 7:09 that evening, Chief Justice Harlan F. Stone swore Harry S. Truman into office. Looking on were his wife of twenty-five years, Bess, and their only child, twenty-one-year-old Margaret.

Elizabeth Virginia, known as "Bess," was the oldest of five children. She was born in Independence, Missouri, on February 13, 1885, to Madge Gates and David Wallace. Athletic and outgoing, Bess enjoyed playing basketball, tennis, and baseball. It was in Sunday school in 1890 that six-year-old Harry Truman met the love of his life, five-year-old Bess. They both graduated from Independence High School but didn't start dating until 1910, when they were in their mid-twenties. The couple became engaged in 1917 and were married on June 28, 1919, after Harry returned from service in World War I.

Harry and his partner ran the Truman and Jacobson Haberdashery, a clothing store in Harry's hometown of Independence. After the business went bankrupt in 1922, he entered the political arena with a local judgeship. In 1934, he was elected to the U.S. Senate. Bess worked in his Senate office as a secretary, doing research and escorting constituents around Washington. Although it was common practice to put family members on the payroll, the famous writer Claire Booth Luce accused the Trumans of being unethical and referred to Mrs. Truman as "Payroll Bess." Harry replied in a scathing letter that his wife earned every penny she was paid. In 1944, President Franklin D. Roosevelt chose Harry Truman, the senator from Missouri, as his running mate for his unprecedented fourth term. Truman was sworn in as vice president on January 20, 1945. Three months later, after the sudden death of Franklin Roosevelt, Harry Truman became America's thirty-third president.

As the nation mourned the death of President Roosevelt, the Trumans—including their daughter, Margaret—relocated from a three-bedroom Washington apartment to the White House. After twenty army trucks moved the Roosevelts' twelve-year accumulation of personal belongings out of the White House, the building seemed almost bare, and Mrs. Truman worked with a professional to redecorate it. The family rooms were painted, art was borrowed from the National Gallery, draperies were cleaned, and furniture was reupholstered. On the second floor on the south side of the White House, President Truman had a balcony built overlooking the expansive back lawn. The Trumans enjoyed dining on the lofty perch (which would become known as the Truman Balcony) until they realized they had no privacy from tourists, who would watch them from the street.

In contrast to the previous first lady, the very private Bess Truman refused to give interviews. While Eleanor Roosevelt had gladly chatted with reporters, Mrs. Truman's standard reply to any

question was "No comment." The Trumans were an unpretentious family and treated everyone on the White House staff with respect. Mrs. Truman showed the maids various courtesies, including giving them Sunday evenings off. Whenever a staff member entered a room, the Trumans would introduce that person to their guest. During the Trumans' time in the White House, it became commonplace for a butler or doorman to be presented to a king or prime minister.

Entertaining during the first part of Truman's administration was kept to a minimum because of

ABOVE: *Bess Truman was an avid baseball fan, attending as many Washington Senators games as she could fit into her schedule. When she was not able to attend a game, she listened to the play-by-play on the radio.*

ABOVE: *Margaret and Bess Truman pose in the Blair House. Margaret was a talented singer who made appearances with the National Symphony Orchestra at Constitution Hall in Washington and at Carnegie Hall in New York.*

luncheons, and stood in receiving lines to shake thousands of hands.

Between 1948 and 1952, the White House underwent a massive transformation, brought about by President Truman's horror at discovering that Margaret's piano leg had pierced the floor. After the incident, he ordered an investigation and learned that the 150-year-old building was a fire hazard and was about to collapse in on itself. Support beams were cracked, floors sagged, and there was little in the way of interior reinforcement. During the much needed renovation, the Trumans lived across the street at the Blair House, which had been previously used to accommodate guests of the president. This building became their residence for four years while the White House was totally gutted.

The $5.4 million project involved a major overhaul of the structure. Two stories were added to the basement, and a steel skeleton was built eighteen inches (46cm) inside the original sandstone walls to provide adequate support for the building. As many beams, mantels, floors, and other architectural details as could be salvaged were labeled and returned to their original location.

While the White House was being rebuilt, official entertaining was limited because of the size of the Blair House. In order to accommodate the large guest lists, state dinners were held at various Washington hotels. During the Korean conflict, Mrs. Truman hosted afternoon parties for wounded soldiers at the Blair House. During these gatherings, Margaret and her friends delighted the soldiers by serving as waitresses.

The White House renovation was completed in March 1952. When the Trumans moved back in, the Executive Mansion and offices had central air conditioning, modern bathrooms, and built-in closets. Mrs. Truman allowed the Commission on Renovation to decide how to redecorate the mansion, as she was going to be in the White House

the mourning period for Franklin Roosevelt and the wartime food shortages. After the war, however, White House entertaining resumed at the usual level. President Truman delighted in parties, but his introverted wife was comfortable only with her family and close friends. Nonetheless, Bess performed her responsibilities as the nation's hostess with dignity. She dutifully presided over dinners and receptions, christened ships, attended for only another year and she didn't think it fair to impose her preferences and selections upon the incoming first lady.

On December 1, 1952, Mrs. Truman escorted Mamie Eisenhower, wife of the newly elected president, on a private tour of the White House. The following January, the Trumans happily left Washington for their home in Independence, Missouri. Soon after moving, Harry found his wife sitting by the fire and tossing pieces of paper into it. When he discovered that she was burning their letters, he exclaimed, "Bess, think of history!" to which Bess replied, "I have."

The former president died in 1972 at the age of eighty-eight. Bess Truman died in 1982 at the age of ninety-seven, making her the longest-living of all first ladies. Husband and wife are buried next to each other in Independence.

BELOW: *President and Mrs. Truman wave to the thousands of people gathered near the White House on August 14, 1945, in celebration of V-J Day, which brought an end to World War II.*

MAMIE GENEVA DOUD EISENHOWER

November 14, 1896–November 1, 1979

Dwight D. Eisenhower, president 1953–1961

"I have but one career and its name is Ike."

—Mamie Eisenhower

Mamie Geneva Doud, born in Boone, Iowa, was the second of four daughters of Elivera Carlson and John Sheldon Doud. Mamie's father was a successful meat packer, and she grew up in comfortable surroundings, spending winters in San Antonio, Texas, and summers in Denver, Colorado. She attended a number of different schools, including Miss Wolcott's, a fashionable finishing school for Denver's affluent families.

In October 1915, while visiting Fort Sam Houston near San Antonio, Mamie was introduced to Lieutenant Dwight D. Eisenhower, a recent West Point graduate. They were immediately attracted to each other and even though Mamie had a busy socialite schedule, she made time for the handsome young officer, who proposed on Valentine's Day in 1916. Although Mamie's parents liked Dwight, her father warned her of the difficulties that being a military officer's wife would bring. After assuring her parents that she could handle any hardships she might face, Mamie wed Lieutenant Dwight Eisenhower in her parents' Denver home on July 1, 1916.

As the couple dutifully moved from post to post, Mamie earned a reputation for being an exceptional hostess. Dwight was greatly disappointed not to have received an overseas tour of duty during World War I and felt that he was not getting challenging assignments or the advancements in rank he expected. But great joy was brought into his and Mamie's lives with the birth of their first son, Doud Dwight Eisenhower, called "Icky." Sadly, however, in January 1921, the beloved son died after contracting scarlet fever. Grief and guilt over their child's death caused a rift in the couple's marriage, which almost ended in divorce. Ultimately, Mamie and Dwight reconciled, and in 1922, Mamie gave birth to another son, John.

Although Eisenhower had been disappointed early in his military career, World War II brought him national recognition as he rose to supreme allied commander and five-star general. After the war, he served as president of Columbia University and then supreme commander of the North Atlantic Treaty Organization (NATO). In 1952, General Eisenhower was elected the thirty-fourth president of the United States.

As first lady, Mamie enjoyed being in charge of the large White House staff, making sure everything ran smoothly and to her liking. Her background as a career military officer's wife proved helpful in her new position. She was adept at organizing state events and made sure the White House was kept spotless. Before big events, she insisted on having a dress rehearsal to ensure that everything would run smoothly. At state dinners, she and the president sat side by side in oversize carved chairs at the head of an E-shaped dining table. Although she was weakened by a heart condition from her childhood, Mamie readily performed the duties of first lady, holding teas, luncheons, and receptions and attending dedication ceremonies.

Mamie had little interest in politics and never interfered in the president's business. She entered

the Oval Office only four times in the eight years that they lived in the White House. While President Eisenhower was an early riser who started his day at 6:00 A.M., Mamie rarely requested her breakfast tray before noon. After having her breakfast served in bed, she would call in the chief usher, housekeeper, and secretaries to go over the day's schedule, approve menus, and give orders, all the while using her bed as her command post. She ordered the staff to use the service elevator instead of the family elevator, and regardless of the weather, the staff was not allowed to walk through the White House to get from one part of the building to another. She abhorred seeing footprints on the carpets, so staff members were constantly vacuuming, then tiptoeing around the edge of the room so as not to make a mark.

Mamie also kept a close eye on the White House budget. She scoured the ads for bargains and sent an unmarked truck and a Secret Service

ABOVE: *Newlyweds Dwight and Mamie Eisenhower are shown in this July 1, 1916, photograph. Although they moved from fort to fort, the hospitable couple's military quarters were always known as "Club Eisenhower."*

RIGHT: *The Eisenhowers celebrate their last Christmas Eve in the White House. The adults, from left to right, are: President Eisenhower's son John, daughter-in-law Barbara Jean, the president, and Mamie Eisenhower. The first couple's grandchildren, from left to right, are: Barbara Ann, David, Mary Jean, and Susan.*

agent into grocery stores to purchase the desired items. Every morning she asked for a list of leftovers. If chicken had been served the previous evening, she ordered the leftovers made into chicken salad for lunch. She also economized by having a friend in Kansas City supply their meat free of charge and having fresh vegetables grown on their own Gettysburg, Pennsylvania, farm delivered to the White House.

Mamie enjoyed entertaining and was creative when it came to decorating for the holidays. St. Patrick's Day meant that the columns were decked out with green ribbons, top hats, and shamrocks. Easter brought butterflies hanging from the chandeliers and fresh flowers filling every nook. On Halloween, the State Dining Room was filled with flying witches, bats, and skeletons hanging from the ceiling, while the grand foyer was festooned with cornstalks and jack-o'-lanterns. It was at Christmas, though, that Mamie really went all out: dozens of decorated trees were stationed throughout the mansion, every window was adorned with a green wreath, and nearly every empty nook was filled with poinsettias.

Although Mamie ran the household in the strict style of a general's wife, she was also kind-hearted. A ground-floor closet was filled with toys that had been donated by a manufacturer, and at Christmastime, she saw that as many underprivileged children as possible received the toys as gifts. She also personally shopped for and handed out Christmas presents to everyone on the staff.

During the early 1950s, television was becoming a staple in American households. Mamie enjoyed the serial *As the World Turns*, rarely missing an installment. She and "Ike" took their evening meals on TV trays while they watched shows such as *I Love Lucy* and *You Bet Your Life*. To relax and get away from Washington, they often spent time at Shangri-La, the presidential retreat in the nearby Maryland

mountains. Mamie had the lodge redecorated, and the president renamed the retreat Camp David in honor of his grandson.

In 1961, after spending eight years in the White House, the Eisenhowers retired to their Gettysburg, Pennsylvania, farm. Dwight died in 1969, and Mamie lived another ten years. She and the former president are buried next to each other in Abilene, Kansas.

ABOVE: *Although she was a grandmother in her late fifties during her White House years, Mamie Eisenhower (pictured here with her husband) projected a youthful and stylish image and regularly appeared on the "Most Admired Women" list.*

JACQUELINE LEE BOUVIER KENNEDY

July 28, 1929–May 19, 1994
John F. Kennedy, president 1961–1963

"If you bungle raising your children, I don't think whatever else you do well matters very much."

—Jacqueline Kennedy

As Jacqueline Lee Bouvier made her debut into society in 1947, Hearst newspaper society columnist Cholly Knickerbocker proclaimed the striking, raven-haired beauty "Queen deb of the year." Jacqueline, the older of two daughters of Janet Lee and stockbroker John "Black Jack" Bouvier III, was born into wealth in July 1929 in Southampton, New York. In 1940, Janet divorced her alcoholic husband and two years later married wealthy stockbroker Hugh Auchincloss. Jacqueline attended exclusive private schools including Miss Porter's School in Farmington, Connecticut, and Vassar College. She attended the Sorbonne in Paris and earned a degree in art from George Washington University in 1951.

In 1952, Jacqueline began working for the *Washington Times-Herald* newspaper as the "Inquiring Camera Girl," interviewing people on the street as well as prominent Washingtonians, such as Pat Nixon. She also interviewed John F. Kennedy, whom she had met in early 1951 thanks to a mutual friendship with Charles Bartlett. John and Jacqueline dated for two and a half years before marrying on September 12, 1953, in Newport, Rhode Island. The ceremony was performed by Archbishop Richard J. Cushing, who read a special blessing on the marriage from Pope Pius XII.

Although Jacqueline had little interest in politics, she openly campaigned for her husband in the

1960 presidential race. Her youth, style, and ability to speak multiple languages impressed voters throughout the nation. On January 20, 1961, at thirty-one, Jacqueline Kennedy became America's first lady.

After the swearing in of John F. Kennedy as America's thirty-fifth president, the Kennedys returned to the White House to celebrate with a large luncheon for the extended family. Jackie, who was still recovering from a cesarean section she had had two months earlier, felt overwhelmed and stayed upstairs alone in the family quarters, agreeing to see only her cousin Michel Bouvier. That evening, after attending two inaugural balls, Jackie collapsed, exhausted.

Americans were taken with the grace and style of the young president's family. The White House radiated with lively dinners attended by glamorous stars, and women all over the country adopted the "Jackie look," which included her signature pillbox hat and two-piece suit. The charming first lady was an immediate success, and the couple's two young children, three-year-old Caroline and two-month-old John Kennedy, Jr., affectionately called "John-John," enchanted the public.

Jackie's art degree and her interest in history were put to good use when she initiated a massive restoration project. Believing that the mansion should reflect the lives of the previous occupants through furniture, paintings, and other objects, she formed a committee made up of museum directors and historians, and she solicited gifts of furnishings with historical value. She also found a treasure trove of furniture in the White House storerooms. Along with researching the history of the furnishings, Jackie supervised the publication of a guidebook titled *The White House: An Historic Guide*, which is still in print. In February 1962, nearly

80 million American television viewers watched the first lady give a room-by-room tour of the newly redecorated mansion.

Not only were the public rooms redone, but the upstairs family quarters received a makeover as well. A kitchen and a family dining area were added, and the walls were filled with original paintings borrowed from the National Gallery of Art. The third-floor solarium—which was outfitted with a sandbox, animal cages, and an aquarium—became a nursery school for Caroline and her classmates. Outside, just beyond the president's West Wing

ABOVE: *Jackie Kennedy, pictured here in August 1960, charmed the nation with her grace and style. During the presidential campaign of that year, her public appearances were limited by her pregnancy. Nonetheless, she actively supported her husband by answering campaign mail, taping television commercials, and writing a syndicated newspaper column entitled "Campaign Wife."*

ABOVE: *Jacqueline Bouvier earned $42.50 per week as the "Inquiring Camera Girl" for the* Washington Times-Herald.

RIGHT: *President-elect and Mrs. Kennedy leave their Georgetown home on January 19, 1961, to attend an inaugural concert. For this event, Jackie wore an ivory silk gown designed by Oleg Cassini. The heavy snow that blanketed the area that evening required hundreds of trucks and plows to clear the street for the inaugural parade the next day.*

office, were swings, a tree house, a slide, a trampoline, pens for a variety of animals, and a stable for the ponies.

Maintaining privacy and protecting her children were Mrs. Kennedy's top priorities. Caroline and John Jr. were the most photographed children in the country, their pictures running in newspapers, in magazines, and on television news programs. Like Edith Roosevelt had done half a century earlier, Mrs. Kennedy hired a press secretary, who helped her carefully orchestrate what the public was allowed to see of the president's children.

As first lady, Jackie was a valuable asset to her husband. Wherever they traveled—be it India, Pakistan, or France, to name a few—she made a positive impression, charming both the public and prominent statesmen, including Soviet premier

Nikita Khrushchev and French president Charles de Gaulle. When the Kennedys visited France, throngs of people cheered for both the president and the enchanting first lady. Later, at a luncheon during that trip, the president remarked, "I do not think it altogether inappropriate to introduce myself. I am the man who accompanied Jacqueline Kennedy to France."

There was tension in the marriage due to the president's philandering and his exasperation with Jackie's spending habits. In 1961, her expenditures for clothing and other personal items amounted to more than $100,000; in 1962, her annual spending increased to more than $120,000. There is little doubt that Jackie was deeply hurt by her husband's infidelity, and she began to spend more time away from the White House. She made frequent trips to

ABOVE: *On February 14, 1962, CBS television aired a tour of the newly redecorated public rooms of the White House. Nearly 80 million Americans tuned in to the broadcast.*

Palm Beach, New York, and Hyannis Port in addition to vacationing abroad in Italy and Greece.

The death of the couple's newborn son Patrick Bouvier Kennedy in August 1963 seemed to bring husband and wife closer than they had been in a long time. When the president asked Jackie to accompany him on a campaign trip to Texas in November, she readily agreed.

On November 22, 1963, the president's motorcade made its way through the streets of Dallas, where the Kennedys were greeted by thousands of people who lined the roadways, waving and cheering. But the jubilance of the day was brought to an abrupt end with the assassination of President Kennedy, who was shot as Jackie was seated beside him. Only two hours later aboard Air Force One, Jacqueline Kennedy, still wearing her bloodstained pink suit, stood next to Lyndon Johnson as he was sworn in as America's thirty-sixth president. Before leaving the White House, Jackie requested that a

152

LEFT, TOP: *Caroline and John Jr. were the darlings of the American public. When a reporter once spotted Caroline at the White House and asked her where her father was, the young girl (only three years old at the time) responded, "He's upstairs with his shoes and socks off, doing nothing." Here, Caroline sits atop her pony "Macaroni," a present from Lyndon Johnson; her parents and younger brother look on.*

LEFT, BOTTOM: *In June 1962, Jackie Kennedy visited the National Institute for the Protection of Children in Mexico City. Here, she distributes gifts to abandoned children who were helped by the Institute.*

plaque be made to be placed in the Lincoln Bedroom, which she had shared with her husband. The plaque was commissioned with the inscription: "In this room lived John Fitzgerald Kennedy with his wife Jacqueline during the two years, ten months and two days he was President of the United States."

During her post–White House years, Jackie helped establish the John F. Kennedy Library and Museum in Boston and the Kennedy Center for the Performing Arts in Washington. In 1968, she married Greek shipping magnate Aristotle Onassis. After Onassis' death in 1975, Jackie moved permanently to New York City, where she became an editor at Doubleday. On May 19, 1994, she lost her battle with cancer. She was laid to rest next to President Kennedy in Arlington National Cemetery.

CLAUDIA ALTA (LADY BIRD) TAYLOR JOHNSON

b. December 12, 1912

Lyndon B. Johnson, president 1963–1969

"Anything that's done here, or needs to be done, remember this: my husband comes first, the girls second, and I will be satisfied with what's left."

—*Lady Bird Johnson to White House Chief Usher J.B. West*

Claudia Taylor—born in Karnack, Texas, in 1912—was the only child of Thomas Jefferson Taylor, a local merchant, and Minnie Lee Pattillo. Claudia's nursemaid, Alice Tittle, commented that the young girl was "as purty as a little lady bird." The nickname stuck, and Claudia has been Lady Bird ever since. When she was only five years old, Lady Bird lost her mother, at which point her aunt Effie Pattillo moved from Alabama to help take care of her.

In 1933, Lady Bird received a degree in journalism from the University of Texas. In September 1934, she met Lyndon B. Johnson, who was an aide to Congressman Dick Kleberg of Texas at the time. Only two months after making each other's acquaintance, the couple became husband and wife on November 17.

Lyndon Johnson had a long political career. He was elected to Congress in 1937 and to the Senate in 1948. In 1960, when he was running for vice president, Lady Bird traveled more than thirty-five thousand miles (56,315km) campaigning on behalf of the Kennedy-Johnson ticket. Her hard work paid off when the Democrats won. Robert Kennedy always claimed that it was Lady Bird who had carried Texas in that election.

On November 22, 1963, Vice President Johnson and Lady Bird were riding two cars behind the president and first lady in the Dallas, Texas, motorcade when Kennedy was assassinated. Only two hours later onboard Air Force One, U.S. District Court Judge Sarah T. Hughes administered the presidential oath to Lyndon Johnson. Lady Bird looked on while her husband was sworn in as America's thirty-sixth president.

Moving into the White House in December 1963 was a somber occasion. The Johnsons were supportive of Jackie Kennedy and allowed her as much time as she needed to make a smooth transition for her children. Caroline Kennedy's third-floor schoolroom remained in operation until the semester ended in mid-January. Upon taking over the role of first lady, Lady Bird continued the White House restoration project begun by Jackie and insisted that the mansion be maintained in perpetuity as a museum. She convinced the president to issue an executive order providing for a permanent curator and establishing the Committee for the Preservation of the White House.

Lady Bird's primary concern was to make the 132-room mansion a place where her husband could work comfortably. Her second concern was to make the White House a home for her family. The Johnsons' two daughters livened up the White House with dances and parties. Playful and friendly, Luci, the younger girl, was always teasing the Secret Service agents assigned to her. And Lynda, who transferred from the University of Texas to George Washington University, practically changed the family quarters into a makeshift college dormitory.

The Johnsons entertained often, hosting barbecues, carnivals, receptions, and dinners. To make sure that they could accommodate last-minute

guests, they kept the White House staff perpetually on standby (on one occasion, the president spontaneously invited all of Congress for lunch). Lady Bird soon found that a new set of china was required because of the increasing number of people attending state dinners. The new state service, which included 216 place settings, was designed by Tiffany and Company, produced by Castleton China of New Castle, Pennsylvania, and paid for by an anonymous donor. The dinner plates featured an eagle and a border of flowers, while each dessert plate bore an official state flower—

ABOVE: *Lady Bird Johnson was devoted to her husband, and he to her. The couple would openly walk around the White House grounds holding hands. President Johnson often remarked to reporters, "I don't know how I deserved a lady like Lady Bird."*

RIGHT: *The wedding of Luci Baines Johnson and Patrick John Nugent on August 6, 1966, was an extravaganza televised by all three major networks. A choir consisting of one hundred members sang as Luci walked down the aisle at the Shrine of the Immaculate Conception in Washington, D.C. Here, the newlyweds cut into their three-hundred-pound (112kg), seven-tiered wedding cake, as President and Mrs. Johnson look on.*

BELOW: *Always a strong advocate for the environment and beautification, Lady Bird Johnson called upon friends to plant thousands of daffodils and tulips in the nation's capital. In 1966, she received the George Foster Peabody award for the television special "A Visit to Washington with Mrs. Lyndon B. Johnson on Behalf of a More Beautiful America."*

all fifty states and the District of Columbia were represented. Among the most memorable social events during Lady Bird's tenure as first lady were a dinner given in honor of Princess Margaret and her husband, Lord Snowdon, in November 1965 and the weddings of the Johnsons' daughters, Luci and Lynda, in 1966 and 1967, respectively.

As first lady, Mrs. Johnson took on several projects. She traveled around the country, meeting people and reporting back to the president on his war against poverty. She also held luncheons for female leaders; for these events, she selected a topic of discussion and invited professional women—from actresses and lawyers to journalists and elected officials—to lead the discussion. A strong

proponent of women's issues, Lady Bird would say to her husband from time to time, "Well, what did you do for women today?" The president valued Lady Bird's opinions and supported her causes, including the Highway Beautification Act. The bill, which limited billboards on federal highways, was passed in 1965. In general, Lady Bird was a strong advocate for the environment and directed much of her energy toward the preservation of America's scenic beauty.

When it came time for President Johnson to campaign for reelection, he was told that it would not be safe for him to do so in the South because of his support of civil rights legislation. Since it was inadvisable for him to go, President Johnson asked Lady Bird to campaign for him there instead, and she readily agreed. During 1964, Lady Bird visited eight states on a 1,682-mile (2,706km) whistle-stop tour from Washington to New Orleans. The train campaign—called "the Lady Bird Special"—was an overwhelming success, and Johnson won the race for office. On January 20, 1965, Lady Bird held an open Bible for her husband as he was sworn into office; she was the first wife of a president to do so.

Despite Lyndon Johnson's success in 1964, his approval rating plummeted as the war in Vietnam escalated, and he decided not to run for reelection in 1968. After his term came to an end, he and Lady Bird retired to their ranch in Texas, where they lived together until his death in 1973. During her post–White House years, Lady Bird has been active on behalf of a number of important causes. She has served on various boards and promoted the arts and education. Today, she continues her work for the environment and promotes education through the Lyndon Baines Johnson Library and Museum.

LEFT: *This radiant yellow gown, designed by John Moore of New York, was worn by Lady Bird Johnson at her husband's inaugural ball in 1965. Made of double-woven satin, the floor-length dress features a bateau neckline and delicate cap sleeves.*

PATRICIA RYAN NIXON

March 16, 1912–June 22, 1993

Richard M. Nixon, president 1969–1974

"Being First Lady is the hardest unpaid job in the world."

—*Patricia Nixon*

Thelma Catherine Ryan was born on March 16, 1912, in Ely, Nevada, to Kate Halberstadt Bender and her Irish immigrant husband, Will Ryan. Thrilled to have a daughter born just moments before St. Patrick's Day, Will called the little girl his "Saint Patrick's babe in the morning," which ultimately transformed into "Pat." The family even celebrated her birthday on St. Patrick's Day, though she was actually born the day before.

When Pat was two years old, the Ryan family moved to a small farm just outside Los Angeles. As she grew older, she helped out around the farm, driving the team of horses and the tractor and picking vegetables. When she was thirteen, her mother died, at which point Pat took over the household chores as well. Tragedy struck again five years later with the death of her beloved, gruff father, who had fallen ill with tuberculosis. Pat and her two older brothers worked together to keep the farm and put one another through school. Pat took employment at a bank as a bookkeeper and janitor, and Bill ran the farm. Tom—the first to go to college—attended the University of Southern California on a football scholarship; he also worked at Universal Studios and as a soda jerk.

Pat desperately missed her father. To honor him and his Irish heritage, she formally changed her first name to Patricia. She continued to work once she entered college, taking various jobs, one of which was as an extra in a movie. In 1937, she graduated from the University of Southern California cum laude.

After graduation, Pat taught high school in Whittier, California. In her free time, she enjoyed performing in amateur theater. In fact, it was this passion that led her to meet Richard Nixon, a lawyer at the time, who was cast opposite her in a community production. He was immediately taken with the lovely young teacher and told her he was going to marry her someday. On June 21, 1940, at the Mission Inn in Riverside, California, his prediction came true.

Pat was not very enthusiastic when her husband decided to pursue a political career, but she honored his decision. She did make two requests of him, though: that their home would always be a refuge from politics where their children could have a normal life and that she would never be called on to make any political speeches. Her husband agreed to both conditions, though his promises were ultimately forgotten. Although Pat was a reluctant campaigner, she supported Richard by working behind the scenes as he rose in politics from being a congressman to being America's thirty-seventh president.

As first lady, Mrs. Nixon continued the White House restoration work, adding hundreds of paintings and original artifacts to the White House collection. What's more, she improved access to the White House for people with disabilities, opened the mansion for candlelight tours in the evenings, and arranged for the White House to be illuminated at night with floodlights.

The Nixon White House entertained formally with white-tie affairs. The Nixons hosted concerts by American artists who performed everything from opera to bluegrass. Some of the noteworthy entertainers included Isaac Stern, Duke Ellington,

Leonard Bernstein, and Bob Hope. On Sundays, rather than attend a local church, the Nixons hosted a nondenominational service with guest ministers in the East Room.

Pat Nixon used her position as first lady to promote volunteer work. She especially encouraged women to work on political campaigns. In 1969, Pat toured the United States, visiting various community projects that helped the poor, elderly, and handicapped. She had traveled extensively with her husband when he was vice president under Eisenhower and continued to do so when he

ABOVE: *Pat Nixon did a lot of traveling with and on behalf of her husband. Here, she addresses a crowd in McLean, Virginia, the first stop on a five-state tour in 1971 to see the results of President Nixon's Legacy of Parks program. The program eventually turned fifty thousand acres of federal property into parklands and brought increased recreational opportunities into cities.*

RIGHT, TOP: *During the presidential trip to Vietnam in 1969, Pat Nixon visited the 24th Evacuation Hospital, just north of Saigon. When officials offered to show her around the hospital, the first lady commented, "I don't really want to learn about the hospital, I came to see the boys."*

RIGHT, BOTTOM: *During President and Mrs. Nixon's groundbreaking visit to China in 1972, the first lady told Premier Chou En-lai how much she enjoyed seeing the pandas at the Peking Zoo. In response, he promised to give her some. Within a matter of months, two giant pandas named Ling-Ling and Hsing-Hsing arrived at the National Zoo, where they were a major tourist attraction for many years.*

OPPOSITE: *Pat Nixon wore this gown, designed by Adele Simpson of New York, to the inaugural ball on January 20, 1973, at the beginning of her husband's second term as chief executive. The dress, which features turquoise silk organza over turquoise and silver silk lamé, is on display at the Richard Nixon Library and Birthplace in Yorba Linda, California.*

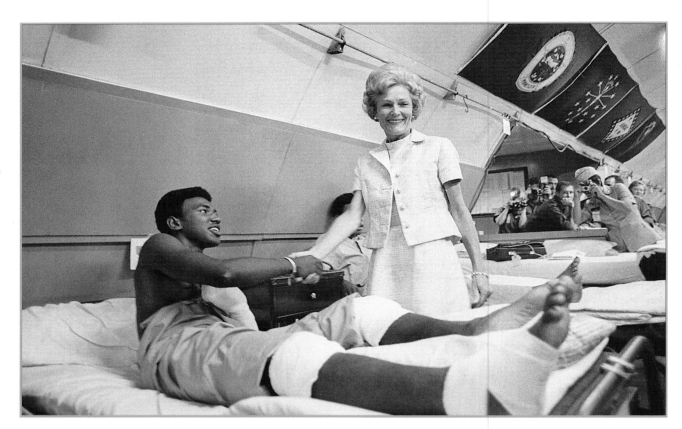

became president, accompanying him on his
widely publicized tour of China and to the Soviet
Union, as well as traveling on her own to Africa
and South America; in 1970, acting as a goodwill
ambassador, she flew to Peru with relief supplies
for earthquake victims there.

In June 1971, the Nixons' older daughter,
Tricia, became the first president's daughter to be
married in the Rose Garden. Hoping for a clear
day, the family did not have a tent set up in case of
inclement weather. Unfortunately, the day turned
out to be gray and rainy. Pat paced the floor with
her younger daughter, Julie Nixon Eisenhower,
repeatedly looking up at the threatening sky.
Knowing that her daughter would be crushed not
to have her dream wedding in the Rose Garden,
she left the decision of whether or not to move the
ceremony indoors to Tricia, who in turn appealed
to her father to consult the air force weather station.
The president heeded her request and was told
that there would be a fifteen-minute break in the
clouds over Washington at 4:30 P.M. So the four
o'clock wedding was delayed for thirty minutes,
and at exactly 4:30 the sun came out as the bride
walked down the Rose Garden path on the arm of
her father. Shortly after the groom, Edward Cox,
kissed his bride, the rain resumed.

During the difficult days of the Watergate
scandal, Mrs. Nixon stood by her husband. She
hoped he would continue to fight the impeachment charges, but when he chose to resign, she
supported his decision. After the couple left the
White House in August 1974, they enjoyed a quiet
retirement at their San Clemente, California, estate.
In 1980, they moved to New York City and later
to Park Ridge, New Jersey, where the former first
lady died on June 22, 1993, at the age of eighty-
one. Her husband followed her ten months later.
The couple are buried at the Richard Nixon
Library and Birthplace in Yorba Linda, California.

ELIZABETH BLOOMER FORD

b. April 18, 1918

Gerald R. Ford, president 1974–1977

"I do not believe that being first lady should prevent me from expressing my views."

—Betty Ford

Born in Chicago on April 18, 1918, to Hortense Neahr and William S. Bloomer, Elizabeth (Betty) Ann Bloomer was raised in Grand Rapids, Michigan. As a young girl, Betty loved to dance, a passion that she continued to follow as she grew up. After finishing high school, she attended the Bennington School of Dance in Vermont. Later, she headed to New York, where she joined the renowned dance troupe of Martha Graham and worked as a Powers model. In 1941, Betty moved back to her hometown of Grand Rapids and became a fashion coordinator for Herpolsheimer's Department Store. The following year, she married William C. Warren, but they were divorced in 1947.

That same year, Betty was introduced to Gerald Ford, a local lawyer and former University of Michigan football star. They dated regularly and on October 15, 1948, exchanged marital vows. Only a couple of weeks later, Gerald Ford was elected to the House of Representatives.

Betty deftly balanced the responsibility of raising four children with the obligations of being a congressman's wife. She volunteered with the Cub Scouts and the PTA, taught Sunday school, participated in the Congressional Wives Club, and helped out in her husband's office whenever needed. In August 1964, she suffered a pinched nerve in her neck while trying to raise a window. Although she spent weeks in the hospital, she didn't fully recover.

LEFT: *Betty Ford was the most outspoken first lady since Eleanor Roosevelt. Although her public frankness brought some criticism, her approval ratings in the press and public opinion polls remained high. Her honesty about her personal troubles made it easier for many Americans with similar problems to seek treatment.*

RIGHT: *Betty Ford stands by her husband as he is sworn in as the thirty-eighth president of the United States by Chief Justice Warren E. Burger.*

The injury developed into arthritis and led to her dependency on painkillers. By 1974, thanks to physical therapy and psychological counseling, Betty was able to give up the painkillers.

After the resignation of Vice President Spiro Agnew in October 1973, President Richard Nixon named Gerald Ford his new vice president. Less than a year later, on August 9, 1974, President Nixon resigned from office, making Gerald Ford America's thirty-eighth president.

Betty Ford was easily was one of America's most outspoken first ladies. She readily offered her opinions on all sorts of subjects, from the legalization of abortion to the Equal Rights Amendment, both of which she supported. A strong advocate of women's rights, she encouraged her husband to appoint women to cabinet positions, the Supreme Court, and the Foreign Service (President Ford appointed Carla Hill as secretary of health and education and Ann Armstrong as ambassador to

Britain). Betty visited sick children in area hospitals and pushed for improved conditions in nursing homes. She also promoted the arts and humanities in the White House.

In September 1974, Betty had a radical mastectomy. Her openness about her fight with cancer encouraged women all over the country to get breast exams. Marguerite "Happy" Rockefeller, wife of Vice President Nelson Rockefeller, also had breast cancer and credited Betty Ford with saving her life.

In August 1975, Betty Ford was interviewed by reporter Morley Safer on the CBS news program *60 Minutes*. Her candor about abortion, premarital sex, and marijuana caused a flood of angry letters to pour into the White House. Despite the outcry, polls showed that most Americans appreciated her honesty, and she became one of the most admired women in the country. When the editors of *Newsweek* named her Woman of the Year, they singled out her frankness as her most valuable asset.

LEFT, TOP: *President Ford visits his wife in the Bethesda Naval Hospital in October 1974 as she recovers from a mastectomy. Betty humanized the role of first lady by openly discussing breast cancer, as well as drug and alcohol addiction, and showing that her family struggled with the same problems as average American families.*

LEFT, BOTTOM: *Betty Ford, who championed women's issues, saw no contradiction in the fact that she supported the Equal Rights Amendment and made her family her top priority. She felt that downgrading the work of housewives undervalued women's talents in all areas. Speaking at the International Women's Year Conference in October 1975, the first lady stated, "The long road to equality rests on achievements of women and men in altering how women are treated in every area of everyday life."*

During the presidential race of 1976, Betty's popularity was evident. There were not only Jerry Ford political buttons, but Betty Ford ones as well. Some of the most popular read "Keep Betty in the White House" and "Betty's Husband for President."

After President Ford was defeated by Jimmy Carter, the Fords moved to a large ranch house in Palm Springs, California. Betty developed osteoarthritis and once again became dependent on painkillers, as well as alcohol. Acknowledging her problem, Betty admitted herself to the Long Beach Naval Hospital for treatment in 1978. In a press statement, she spoke of her addiction and urged people with similar problems to seek professional help. Adamant that others receive the necessary help for chemical dependency, she founded, along with Leonard Firestone, the Betty Ford Center in Rancho Mirage, California, which opened in 1982.

ELEANOR ROSALYNN SMITH CARTER

b. August 18, 1927

Jimmy Carter, president 1977–1981

"I've had tremendous respect for the first lady since I observed

Rosalynn Carter. It's an almost impossible role."

—Jody Powell, President Jimmy Carter's press secretary

OPPOSITE: *Rosalynn Carter overtly portrayed herself as her husband's political partner by attending cabinet meetings and scheduling weekly political lunches with the president. Press secretary Jody Powell noted, "It was not a case of Jimmy Carter doing it with a supportive wife. It had been Jimmy Carter and Rosalynn Carter doing it together as a team."*

Rosalynn Smith was born in Plains, Georgia, in August 1927. Her mother, Frances Allethea (Allie) Murray, was a seamstress, and her father, Wilburn Edgar Smith, was a car mechanic who died when Rosalynn was a teenager. To help the family financially, Rosalynn assisted with her mother's sewing business and worked in a beauty parlor. Despite these responsibilities, she managed to be valedictorian of her class when she graduated from Plains High School in 1945. She went on to attend Georgia Southwestern College.

Rosalynn came to know her husband-to-be through her friend Ruth Carter, sister of Jimmy Carter. The two went on their first date when Jimmy was home on vacation from the United States Naval Academy. On July 7, 1946, the two were married at the Plains Methodist Church.

Rosalynn happily moved away from the small town of Plains. She enjoyed living on remote bases as the wife of a naval officer, a position that took them to a number of different locations. When Jimmy's father died in 1953, he resigned his naval commission—a decision that disappointed Rosalynn—in order to go back to Plains to manage the family peanut business. Upon their return, Rosalynn, who was the mother of three young sons by this point, started working in the business as a bookkeeper. The couple would have one more child, Amy Lynn, in 1967.

When Jimmy entered politics in 1962, Rosalynn readily campaigned for him. She made appearances at barbecues, chicken processing plants, and rattlesnake roundups. After Jimmy served in the Georgia state senate, he went on to become governor in 1971. As first lady of Georgia, Rosalynn visited every mental hospital in the state and served as honorary chairperson of the Georgia Special Olympics. When her husband ran for president in 1976, she set out on the campaign trail once again, helping her husband to achieve his narrow victory over incumbent Gerald Ford. After Jimmy Carter was sworn in as America's thirty-ninth president, Rosalynn and Jimmy walked the entire mile-and-a-half (2.5km) parade route from the Capitol to the White House, making them the first presidential couple to do so.

A highly active first lady, Rosalynn attended cabinet meetings and traveled around the world on behalf of her husband. She continued her work on behalf of mental health and promoted the ERA. During her first two years in the White House, she visited eighteen countries and more than two dozen American cities, held more than twenty press conferences, and presided over more than eighty official functions.

In 1979 Rosalynn toured Cambodian refugee camps in Thailand, then worked to improve conditions for the Cambodians. At home, she served as honorary chair of the President's Commission on Mental Health. As such, she lobbied for the passage of the Mental Health Systems Act—which provided for an overhaul of national mental health policy—testifying before Congress and helping to draft legislation that added $47 million for mental

health research. Thanks to the commission, the act was approved in September 1980.

Rosalynn also devoted time and energy to the White House preservation effort and to the arts. So that future administrations would not be dependent upon loans from museums and private collections, she worked with the Committee for the Preservation of the White House to establish a trust fund that would procure a permanent collection of American art. She also invited artists such as

RIGHT: *Rosalynn Carter first wore this ensemble—consisting of a blue chiffon dress paired with a sleeveless coat—to the governor's inaugural ball in 1971, when her husband became governor of Georgia. Both garments are trimmed in gold embroidery. Because of the outfit's sentimental value, Rosalynn also wore it to the presidential inaugural ball in 1977.*

OPPOSITE, TOP: *After Jimmy Carter was sworn in as America's thirty-ninth president, he and Rosalynn led the inaugural parade from the Capitol to the White House. This marked the first time that a newly sworn-in president walked the entire length of the parade route.*

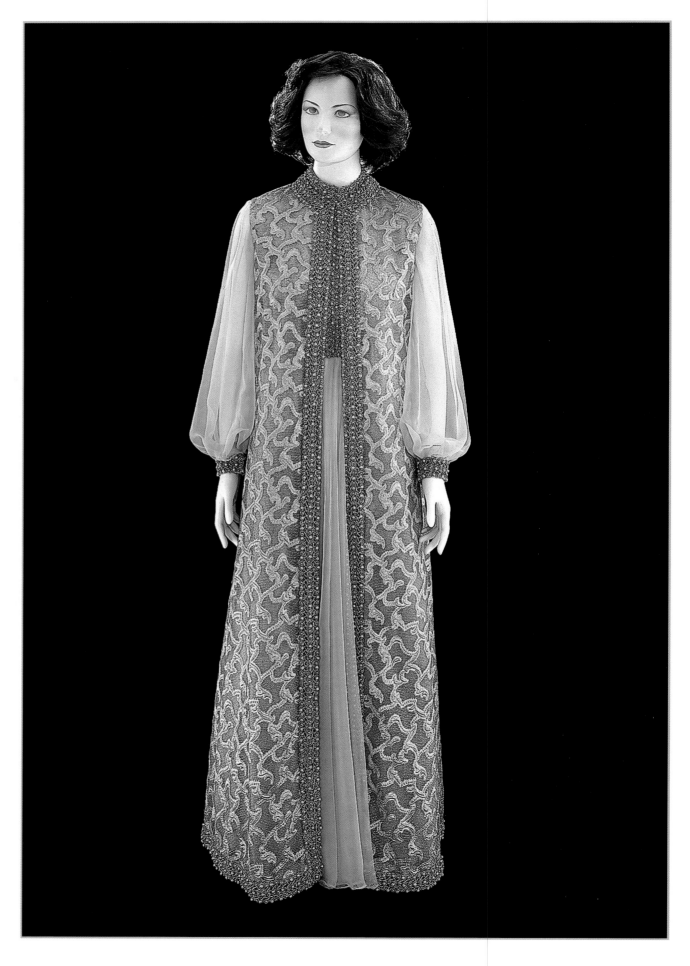

Vladimir Horowitz and Mstislav Rostropovich to entertain at the White House and had their performances broadcast on PBS so that all Americans could enjoy their music.

When the nation was in the midst of an energy crisis in the late 1970s, President Carter appealed to Americans to turn down their thermostats to 65 degrees Fahrenheit (18°C) during the day and 55 degrees Fahrenheit (13°C) at night. Rosalynn pleaded with her husband to turn up the heat in the White House because her offices were so cold that her staff was typing while wearing gloves. The president, however, was determined to set a good example for the country and denied her request.

President Carter solicited his wife's opinion in nearly every decision he made. In fact, Rosalynn was frequently criticized for the close partnership that they shared. She also received criticism for attending cabinet meetings and representing her husband throughout the world as his unofficial ambassador. During the Camp David peace accords between Israeli prime minister Menachem Begin and Egyptian president Anwar Sadat, Rosalynn sat in on most of the negotiations, taking more than two hundred pages of notes. After the signing of the peace treaty on March 26, 1979, Rosalynn celebrated the accomplishment by hosting a dinner for 1,800 people on the South Lawn of the White House.

In November 1979, the Carter administration was faced with one of its most difficult challenges: the taking of American hostages in Tehran. The president refused to leave the White House until the crisis was resolved. He spent the next year negotiating for their release, leaving Rosalynn to campaign for his reelection. During the 1980 race for office, the first lady traveled around the country, defending her husband's policies and reassuring people that the president was healthy and in command. Although she campaigned vigorously, Carter lost the election to Ronald Reagan.

BELOW: *Rosalynn Carter shakes hands with President Anwar Sadat in September 1978 at Camp David. In the background are Prime Minister Menachem Begin and President Jimmy Carter. Rosalynn's journal of the two-week Camp David summit totaled more than two hundred pages and is considered the best record of personal interactions at that historic meeting.*

After leaving the White House in 1981, Rosalynn helped establish the Carter Presidential Center in Atlanta. Her best-selling autobiography, *First Lady from Plains*, was published in 1984. Today, she works alongside her husband renovating and building homes with Habitat for Humanity; she also acts as vice chair on the board of trustees for the Carter Center, an Atlanta-based organization that promotes human rights and peace globally. Rosalynn was with her husband in Stockholm when he received the 2002 Nobel Peace Prize.

NANCY DAVIS REAGAN

b. July 6, 1921

Ronald Reagan, president 1981–1989

"It's silly to suggest my opinion should not carry some weight with a man

I've been married to for thirty-five years…and I make no apologies

for looking out for his personal and political welfare."

—Nancy Reagan

Anne Frances Robbins, known as "Nancy," was born in New York City in July 1921 to actress Edith Luckett and salesman Kenneth Robbins. The couple divorced shortly after Nancy's birth, and while her mother was traveling with shows, Nancy lived with her aunt and uncle in Maryland. In 1929, Edith married Dr. Loyal Davis, a Chicago neurosurgeon. Nancy adored her stepfather, who adopted her when she was fourteen. Actors and actresses frequently visited the Davis home, and Nancy herself developed the acting bug. In 1943, she graduated from Smith College with a degree in drama. After graduation, Nancy toured with a road company, acted on Broadway, and earned parts in eleven films. In her last movie, *Hellcats of the Navy* (1956), she played opposite her actor husband, Ronald Reagan.

It was in 1949 that Nancy met Ronald Reagan, who was president of the Screen Actors Guild at the time. Three years later, on March 4, 1952, they were married. Within a few years, Nancy retired from acting to become a full-time wife and mother. The couple had two children, Patricia Ann and Ronald Prescott.

When Ronald Reagan decided to run for governor of California, Nancy enthusiastically supported him. He was elected in 1966. Instead of living in the governor's mansion, however, the couple rented a home in a more fashionable part of town. The decision stemmed from the fact that Nancy was appalled at the run-down condition of the governor's mansion, which she referred to as a firetrap, and she refused to raise her children there. Even though the Reagans used their own funds for their housing, Nancy was criticized for the move, which was considered an act of arrogance. However, after she took some of the wives of members of the state legislature on a tour of the governor's mansion, they agreed that the house was in deplorable condition. In the end, funds were allocated to renovate the building.

Nancy enjoyed her role as governor's wife. She became active in veterans affairs and in the Foster Grandparent Program, which pairs senior citizens with handicapped children. After Ronald left the governor's office in 1976, he and Nancy began planning his run for the presidency. An integral player in the campaign, Nancy helped choose advisors and made speeches on her husband's behalf. On January 20, 1981, Ronald Wilson Reagan became America's fortieth president.

The Reagans brought glitz and glamour back to the White House. The new tone was evident from the start with the "million-dollar inaugural," so called because of the many wealthy people and celebrities who attended the festivities. When Nancy set about furnishing the private residential area of the White House, she spent the $50,000 allocated by Congress plus an additional $800,000 donated by the Reagans' affluent friends. She also purchased a new set of china for more than $200,000; again, the money was donated by friends.

In general, Nancy received a tremendous amount of criticism for her extravagance. Her critics found fault not only with the huge sums she spent on decorating the White House but also with her acceptance of extremely expensive gowns and jewelry as gifts from designers. When American housewives wrote to the White House asking for the first lady's favorite recipes, they were sent ones that included lobster. All this was happening while America was in a recession and the president was calling upon the country for sacrifices and counting ketchup as a vegetable in lunch menus for

ABOVE: *Nancy Reagan said that her life really began when she married her husband. She was once told she should stop looking at the president as if he were her hero, to which she replied, "But he is my hero!" The Gallup Poll listed her as the number one most admired woman in the world in 1981, 1985, and 1987.*

RIGHT: *Actress Nancy Davis Reagan portrayed navy nurse Helen Blair in the 1957 film* Hellcats of the Navy. *Her husband, Ronald Reagan, starred opposite her in the role of Casey Abbott, commander of a World War II submarine.*

COLUMBIA PICTURES presents
HELLCATS OF THE NAVY
starring **RONALD REGAN**
co-starring NANCY DAVIS, ARTHUR FRANZ
A MORNINGSIDE PRODUCTION

Copyright 1957, Columbia Pictures Corp. Permission granted for Newspaper and Magazine reproduction. (Made in U.S.A.)

"Property of National Screen Service Corp. Licensed for display only in connection with the exhibition of this picture at your theatre. Must be returned immediately thereafter."

57/160

LEFT: *This photograph shows President and Mrs. Reagan standing in the Red Room on the evening of January 20, 1981. Nancy's inaugural gown, designed by James Galanos of Beverly Hills, features white lace laid over silk and embroidered with crystals and beads. Nancy received much criticism for her opulent taste in dress and entertaining. Television personality Johnny Carson joked that Nancy's favorite junk food was caviar. At an affair in New York, Nancy herself quipped that all the talk referring to her as Queen Nancy was ridiculous, as she would never wear a crown because it would mess up her hair.*

underprivileged children. In 1982, to downplay the effect of her negative publicity, Nancy did a skit for the Washington Press Club's annual Gridiron Dinner. Decked out in pantaloons, yellow rain boots, a shabby cotton print housedress, a straw hat, and a tattered boa, she sang a self-deprecating rendition of "Secondhand Rose," making fun of herself and her extravagances to the delight of her audience.

But Nancy Reagan was concerned not only with fashion and decor. In fact, she was a champion of many social causes. As first lady, she continued to promote the Foster Grandparent Program, writing a book on the subject titled *To Love a Child*, which was coauthored by Jane Wilkie and published in 1982. In honor of the program, Nancy's friend Frank Sinatra recorded a song with the same title. Proceeds from both song and book were donated to the Foster Grandparent Program. Nancy was also highly active in fighting substance abuse among young people. With her "Just Say No" campaign, she traveled across the country visiting rehabilitation centers and making speeches. She even made a guest appearance on the sitcom *Diff'rent Strokes* in an effort to get her message across to a large young audience.

OPPOSITE, BOTTOM: *In March 1983, Nancy Reagan made a guest appearance on the popular prime-time situation comedy* **Diff'rent Strokes,** *starring* **Gary Coleman.** *With Nancy's endorsement, "Just Say No" clubs sprang up around the country. These clubs are still active today, bringing drug education and peer counseling to children in elementary and middle school.*

LEFT: *Nancy Reagan commissioned a new state service featuring her trademark color—red. The china was made by Lenox in 1981 and includes 220 nineteen-piece place settings.*

Critics accused Nancy of wielding too much power in her husband's administration. Undeniably, she was instrumental in selecting staff and cabinet members. She was also shown on television prompting her husband with responses to questions by reporters. And she played a large part in the firing of Donald Regan, Reagan's chief of staff.

In 1987, Nancy underwent a mastectomy for breast cancer. She said that her choice not to have the less disfiguring lumpectomy was based on her commitment to perform her duties as first lady; her most important responsibility was protecting her husband, and she realized that by having a

lumpectomy and undergoing the necessary follow-up radiation treatment, she would not be available to help him and defend him from the press and his critics.

After two terms in the White House, the Reagans retired to a home in Bel Air, California, another gift from friends. In the autumn of 1989, Nancy's book *My Turn*, about her tenure in the White House, was published. She also established the Nancy Reagan Foundation, which continues to educate people about the hazards of drug abuse. Today, Nancy lives a private life with her husband, who has been diagnosed with Alzheimer's disease.

BARBARA PIERCE BUSH

b. June 8, 1925
George H. W. Bush, president 1989–1993

"In a world where there's AIDS, the homeless, and drugs, if you wear the same dress twice, it's not important. You shouldn't worry about these things. I owe it to the public to look nice and have a clean mind and a clean head of hair. And that's it."

—Barbara Bush

Barbara Pierce was born in Rye, New York, in June 1925 to Pauline Robinson and magazine publisher Marvin Pierce. While she was home during Christmas vacation from Ashley Hall, a boarding school located in South Carolina, Barbara met George Herbert Walker Bush, then a senior at Phillips Academy in Andover, Massachusetts. When George was eighteen years old, he enlisted in the navy, serving as a bomber pilot in the South Pacific during World War II. He and Barbara became husband and wife on January 6, 1945, while he was home on leave.

After the war, George earned a degree from Yale University. The couple then moved to Texas, where George began a career in the oil industry. As he worked his way up in the oil business, Barbara fulfilled the role of a traditional 1950s wife. Between 1946 and 1959, she gave birth to four sons and two daughters. Sadly, their daughter Robin died of leukemia at the age of three.

Barbara supported George in his business endeavors and his decision to enter politics. During his lengthy career in public service, he was a congressman, an ambassador, chairman of the

Republican National Committee, director of the Central Intelligence Agency, and vice president. In 1988, he was elected president of the United States.

The glamour of the Reagan White House was suddenly replaced with muddy dogs and young children. But the American public felt comfortable with the outspoken white-haired grandmother of ten, who was applauded for her forthrightness in dealing head-on with issues and hard-hitting questions. In 1990, Barbara was asked to give the commencement address at Wellesley College. Some of the students protested, saying that the first lady had done nothing

in her own right but be a traditional wife and mother. Despite the objections, Barbara went through with the speech. At the end of her address, she stated to the thousands of people in the crowd, "Who knows, somewhere out there in this audience may even be someone who will one day follow in my footsteps and preside over the White House as the president's spouse. And I wish him well."

As first lady, Barbara devoted much of her time to promoting literacy. She not only visited local schools, where she read to children, but also encouraged citizens to volunteer at schools and other

ABOVE: *Although the job of America's first lady can be trying, it also has its rewards. In her book* Barbara Bush: A Memoir, *the former first lady wrote, "I had the best job in America. Every single day was interesting, rewarding, and sometimes just plain fun."*

RIGHT: *Barbara Bush looks on as U.S. Senate candidate George H.W. Bush receives returns in his first bid for public office in 1964. Although George won the Republican nomination, he was defeated in the general election by incumbent senator Ralph Yarborough.*

Grandma's House and was photographed cuddling a dying baby. This single act changed the way many Americans responded to the disease.

Unlike most other first ladies, Barbara rarely planned any White House entertaining, instead leaving such details to members of the staff. And her style differed dramatically from that of her immediate predecessor. Barbara showed little interest in designer clothes and preferred to purchase her attire off the rack. At her husband's inauguration, Barbara laughed about wearing a pair of $29 shoes. She also joked with reporters about the difference between her and Nancy Reagan's figures, saying, "She wears a size three…so's my leg."

Since leaving the White House in 1993, Barbara has remained highly active. She wrote *Millie's Book: As Dictated to Barbara Bush*, which tells of

organizations that teach children and adults to read. In 1989, she helped establish the Barbara Bush Foundation for Family Literacy. Barbara did not limit all of her efforts to this cause, though. She was active on behalf of the elderly, the homeless, cancer research, and people with AIDS. When she learned that many babies born with AIDS were abandoned at local Washington hospitals and later taken to a place called Grandma's House where they were cared for until they died, she went into action. During a time when AIDS was considered a taboo subject, Mrs. Bush called a press conference at

her pet English springer spaniel's life in the White House, as well as an autobiography titled *Barbara Bush: A Memoir*. She serves as a board member for the Mayo Clinic and works on behalf of several charitable organizations, including the Boys & Girls Clubs of America, the Leukemia Society of America, and Ronald McDonald House. In addition, she continues to be a literacy advocate, acting as honorary chair of the Barbara Bush Foundation for Family Literacy. She and her husband live in Houston, Texas, and spend their summers in Kennebunkport, Maine.

LEFT, TOP: *President and Mrs. Bush smile for the crowd at the inaugural celebration on January 20, 1989. Barbara's gown, designed by Arnold Scaasi, features a velvet bodice with a square neck and a satin dropped-waist skirt with an asymmetrical drape.*

LEFT, BOTTOM: *Barbara Bush called for the compassionate treatment of people with AIDS. When this photograph of her cuddling a baby afflicted with the disease hit newspapers in 1989, it had a powerful impact on the public, altering the way many people viewed the illness.*

HILLARY RODHAM CLINTON

b. October 26, 1947

William J. Clinton, president 1993–2001

"I do get angry about things. I'm not going to deny that . . .
and I'm not at all shy about expressing my opinion."

—*Hillary Clinton in an interview with Barbara Walters, January 12, 1996*

In October 1947, Hillary Rodham was born in Chicago, Illinois, to Hugh E. Rodham, the owner of a textile company, and Dorothy Howell. Growing up in the Chicago suburb of Park Ridge, Hillary was active in the Girl Scouts, sports, and the Methodist Church. On one occasion, the church's youth minister took Hillary and other teens from their white middle-class suburban environment into Chicago, where they visited minority children and gang members. For the first time, Hillary saw the shacks where migrant farm workers lived. That experience was the beginning of her lifelong passion to help children.

In high school, Hillary was a student leader and a member of the National Honor Society. She graduated from Wellesley College in 1969 and gave the class address at commencement. She then went on to earn a law degree from Yale University. It was there that she met fellow student Bill Clinton, whom she married on October 11, 1975, in Fayetteville, Arkansas. After a brief stint teaching at the University of Arkansas Law School, she joined the prestigious Rose Law Firm in 1976. When her husband was elected governor of Arkansas in 1978, Hillary balanced her duties as first lady of the state with motherhood (their daughter, Chelsea, was born in 1980) and a law career devoted to working on behalf of children and families.

During Bill Clinton's bid for the presidency in 1992, he campaigned with his wife as a full partner. "With me, you get two for the price of one" was one of his themes. Hillary also made it perfectly clear that she would be an active partner when her husband became president and that she planned to attend cabinet meetings. When she was attacked for having a career, she angered many homemakers by saying, "I suppose I could have just stayed home and baked cookies and had teas." Political advisors encouraged her to downplay her influence with her husband, soften her hairstyle and overall look, and appear more often in public with Chelsea. In November 1992, William Jefferson Clinton was elected America's forty-second president.

Once in the White House, Hillary Rodham Clinton broke precedent by taking an office in the powerful West Wing instead of the East Wing, which is the traditional realm of the first lady. She chaired the National Commission on Health Care Reform, which raised issues involving affordable health insurance coverage for all Americans, immunizations for children, and public awareness of health concerns. She helped draft legislation for that commission and testified before Congress. Although in the end the health care plan was not passed, Hillary was praised for her hard work and dedication to the proposal.

Hillary achieved a number of significant accomplishments as first lady. She was instrumental in having women appointed to head the Justice Department, Health and Human Services, the Department of Energy, and (in Clinton's second term) the Department of State and Labor. She also worked on behalf of cancer, diabetes, and

osteoporosis research and supported the assault weapons ban. While her frankness and tireless work on behalf of the rights of women and children resulted in criticism from many, she also gained much admiration. She took her concerns to Third World countries, drawing attention to the problems faced by women and children there. In Chile and Nicaragua, she encouraged women to start small businesses by taking advantage of microcredit loans, which made it possible for people too poor to qualify for commercial bank loans

ABOVE: *First lady Hillary Rodham Clinton salutes delegates at the Democratic National Convention in Los Angeles in August 2000. Three months later, she was elected U.S. senator from New York.*

RIGHT: *After graduating from high school in 1965, Hillary Diane Rodham went on to Wellesley College, where she delivered the valedictory address at her commencement in 1969. In that speech, she stated, "The challenge now is to practice politics as the art of making what appears to be impossible, possible."*

FAR RIGHT: *Hillary Clinton wore this sparkling gown, designed by Sarah Phillips, to the 1993 inaugural balls. Made of beaded lace, the violet sheath dress is accented by an organza overskirt.*

OPPOSITE, TOP: *In November 2000, Hillary and daughter Chelsea toured rural villages in Vietnam. During their trip, they observed programs that offer rural women affordable loans enabling them to rise above poverty.*

OPPOSITE, BOTTOM: *Senator Hillary Clinton is shown with Israeli prime minister Ariel Sharon on a visit to Jerusalem in February 2002.*

to borrow money. At the U.N. Conference on Women in 1995, she publicly confronted the Chinese and Indian governments for their blatant violation of human rights in killing women and children. It was also in 1995 that Hillary's book *It Takes a Village and Other Lessons Children Teach Us* was published.

Just as she had done as first lady of Arkansas, Hillary worked tirelessly to balance the duties of first lady of the United States with raising her daughter in the public eye. One day at school, Chelsea broke out with a minor skin rash. The school nurse wanted to give her an over-the-counter antihistamine and told Chelsea she needed permission from one of her parents. Chelsea thought for a moment and said, "You better call my dad because my mom is real busy right now."

Like other contemporary first families, the Clintons promoted the arts in the White House, inviting such celebrities as Isaac Stern and Eric Clapton to perform. Hillary used the White House lawn for formal state dinners, a sculpture exhibition, picnics, and even a carnival. By utilizing this outdoor space, she was able to accommodate many more guests than previous administrations. Believing that the White House belongs to all Americans, Hillary worked with her friend Sharon Rockefeller, president of the PBS affiliate in Washington, to have various performances televised. The events that were selected were designed to appeal to a wide range of tastes. In 1993, C-SPAN broadcast the state dinner in honor of South African president Nelson Mandela. Prior to the dinner, the first lady taped segments that showed much of what putting together such an event entails. The Clintons also allowed lectures that were given in the White House by prominent individuals to be sent by satellite to home computers.

In the midst of all her political and humanitarian activities, Hillary was subject to a number of personal trials and tribulations. There was the Whitewater property scandal, which led to her being subpoenaed by a federal grand jury. And there were the allegations of her husband's indiscretions, as well as his relationship with White House intern Monica Lewinsky, which Hillary was forced to confront in the public spotlight. During the impeachment proceedings against her husband, she publicly showed support for him. Through all of these challenges, Hillary demonstrated strength, poise, and confidence.

On November 7, 2000, Hillary Rodham Clinton was elected U.S. senator for New York, making her the first of the nation's first ladies to hold an elected public office. She and her husband reside in Chappaqua, New York.

LAURA WELCH BUSH

b. November 4, 1946

George W. Bush, president 2001–present

"I have a forum. I won't have it always. The time is now."

—*Laura Bush*

$\mathcal{L}$aura Welch was born in Midland, Texas, on November 4, 1946, to Jenna Hawkins, a bookkeeper, and Harold Welch, a home builder. After receiving a bachelor of science in education from Southern Methodist University in 1968, she worked as a teacher in Dallas and Houston. In 1973, she earned a master's degree in library science from the University of Texas. It was through mutual friends that Laura came to know George W. Bush, whom she met in August 1977. The future president was immediately attracted to the introverted librarian. The couple exchanged wedding vows three months later on November 5. In 1981, Laura gave birth to the couple's twin daughters, Barbara and Jenna.

Although Laura had little interest in politics, she supported her husband when he made his first bid for public office in 1978. After he lost this attempt for a congressional seat, George continued to work in the oil industry and became part owner of the Texas Rangers baseball franchise. His second run for political office was successful, culminating in his election as governor of Texas in 1994.

As first lady of Texas, Laura Bush promoted her primary concerns of women's health issues and education. She was instrumental in founding the Texas Book Festival, which celebrates books and authors. Since its inception in 1996, this event has become an annual fund-raiser for Texas public libraries. Laura also organized an early childhood development

initiative working in conjunction with the Barbara Bush Foundation for Family Literacy.

Laura's laid-back style and unabashed pride in her role as a traditional wife became an asset to her husband when he ran for the presidency in 2000. It was not until many weeks after the November election that George W. Bush was declared America's forty-third president.

As first lady of the nation, Laura has continued to promote her interest in early childhood development. In an address to the American Academy of Pediatrics, she urged doctors to

BELOW: *Kennebunkport, Maine, has long been the summer home of the Bush family. George W. Bush and his wife Laura are shown here in 1987 with their twin daughters, Barbara (at left) and Jenna (at right). The girls are named after their grandmothers.*

OPPOSITE, LEFT: *Laura Bush often visits schools to read to young students. The first lady works tirelessly to promote the importance of exposing children to books.*

encourage reading among their young patients. She also developed the Ready to Read, Ready to Learn program. This initiative has two major goals: that all young children are ready to read and learn when they enter their first classroom and that children have well-trained, qualified teachers, especially in the most impoverished neighborhoods. In another step toward the promotion of literacy, Laura launched in 2001, along with the Library of Congress, the first National Book Festival, which showcased authors from across America. She also began a White House literary series that encourages reading by celebrating American writers. Together, President and Mrs. Bush have visited various schools where they read to children. Laura even appeared on a segment of the PBS children's program *Sesame Street* and read to the popular show's characters and audience.

To help parents of young children, the first lady started *Healthy Start, Grow Smart*, a free magazine designed specifically for them. Educating new parents about nutrition and the importance of reading to children, the publication has issues devoted to each of the first twelve months of a baby's life and is published in Spanish and English. The magazine is mailed monthly to women who receive Medicaid services.

Laura Bush has taken her concern for education to an international audience, as well. In May 2002, she traveled to France, Budapest, Hungary, and the Czech Republic to speak out on the importance of education. She continues to promote women's health care issues and works with organizations that provide shelter and clothing to abused women and neglected children.

During the Christmas season of 2002, Laura hosted the children's program at the Children's

National Medical Center in Washington. As the Christmas theme for the White House that year, she selected "all creatures great and small." The mansion was decorated with reproductions of many of the pets of previous administrations. She also hosted a nationally broadcast tour of the decorated White House for cable television, giving Americans the opportunity to view the decorations.

Since the terrorist attacks on September 11, 2001, Laura has done much to bring calm to Americans, especially children. In November 2001, Laura Bush became the first of the nation's first ladies to broadcast a presidential radio address. On this occasion, she spoke out against the Taliban's oppression of women and children in Afghanistan.

In her list of "The 10 Most Fascinating People of 2002," ABC-TV news commentator Barbara Walters named first lady Laura Bush her number one choice. Walters pointed out the first lady's response following the September 11 attacks, describing her as having a calming presence on the nation. Walters also cited the first lady's encouragement toward parents to comfort their children and assure them they are safe.

ABOVE, RIGHT: Laura Bush strolls across the floor on the evening of January 20, 2001, wearing her inaugural gown created by Dallas-based designer Michael Faircloth. The red chantilly lace and silk scoop-neck dress features crystal beading and has a matching coat and bag.

WHITE HOUSE CHRONOLOGY

GEORGE WASHINGTON (1789–1797)
Martha Dandridge Custis Washington

JOHN ADAMS (1797–1801)
Abigail Smith Adams

THOMAS JEFFERSON (1801–1809)
Widowed. Wife Martha Wayles Skelton Jefferson died in 1782. Dolley Madison (wife of James Madison, then secretary of state) performed most hostess duties. Martha Jefferson Randolph and Mary Jefferson Eppes (the two married daughters of Jefferson) sometimes filled in.

JAMES MADISON (1809–1817)
Dolley Payne Todd Madison

JAMES MONROE (1817–1825)
Elizabeth Kortright Monroe. Eliza Monroe Hay and Maria Monroe Gouverneur (married daughters) often filled in for their mother.

JOHN QUINCY ADAMS (1825–1829)
Louisa Catherine Johnson Adams

ANDREW JACKSON (1829–1837)
Widowed. Wife Rachel Donelson Jackson died in 1828—only a few months before Jackson was sworn in as president. Emily Donelson (Rachel's niece) performed some hostess duties until her death in 1836. Sarah Yorke Jackson (the president's daughter-in-law) subsequently filled in.

MARTIN VAN BUREN (1837–1841)
Widowed. Wife Hannah Hoes Van Buren died in 1819. Angelica Singleton Van Buren presided as first lady after her marriage to Abraham Van Buren (Martin's son) in 1838. Prior to that, Dolley Madison stepped in as hostess, as did various wives of friends, cabinet members, and senators.

WILLIAM HENRY HARRISON (1841)
Anna Tuthill Symmes Harrison (though she did not make it to Washington, D.C., before her husband's death, which occurred a month after he took office). During that month, Jane Irwin Harrison (the widow of one of the Harrisons' sons) filled in.

JOHN TYLER (1841–1845)
Letitia Christian Tyler was first lady until her death in 1842. Because Letitia was partially paralyzed from a stroke, her daughter-in-law Priscilla Cooper Tyler stepped in to perform hostess duties. Julia Gardiner Tyler became first lady upon her marriage to President John Tyler on June 26, 1844.

JAMES K. POLK (1845–1849)
Sarah Childress Polk

ZACHARY TAYLOR (1849–1850)
Margaret Mackall Smith Taylor. Because Margaret was chronically ill, her youngest daughter Mary Elizabeth "Betty" Taylor Bliss took over the hostess duties. Varina Howell Davis (friend of the Taylors and wife of their former son-in-law Jefferson Davis) stepped in when Betty was not available.

MILLARD FILLMORE (1850–1853)
Abigail Powers Fillmore. Because of an ankle injury and failing health, Abigail often had her daughter, Mary Abigail "Abby" Fillmore, fill in. Varina Howell Davis, a family friend and the wife of Jefferson Davis (then a U.S. senator), also served as substitute hostess on occasion.

FRANKLIN PIERCE (1853–1857)
Jane Means Appleton Pierce. Because Jane was severely depressed after the death of her eleven-year-old son Benjamin (known as "Bennie"), hostess duties were performed by her aunt Abby Means, Varina Howell Davis (wife of Jefferson Davis, then secretary of war), and various wives of senate and cabinet members.

JAMES BUCHANAN (1857–1861)
Harriet Lane (niece). Buchanan never married.

ABRAHAM LINCOLN (1861–1865)
Mary Todd Lincoln

ANDREW JOHNSON (1865–1869)
Eliza McCardle Johnson. Martha Johnson Patterson filled in for her ailing mother.

ULYSSES S. GRANT (1869–1877)
Julia Dent Grant

RUTHERFORD B. HAYES (1877–1881)
Lucy Ware Webb Hayes

JAMES A. GARFIELD (1881)
Lucretia Rudolph Garfield

CHESTER A. ARTHUR (1881–1885)
Widowed. Wife Ellen Lewis Herndon Arthur died in 1880. Mary Arthur McElroy (President Arthur's sister) helped out for four months a year. A number of former first ladies—namely Julia Tyler, Harriet Lane Johnston, Julia Grant, and Lucy Hayes—performed hostess duties, as did various wives of friends, senators, and cabinet members.

GROVER CLEVELAND (1885–1889)
Frances Folsom Cleveland (upon her marriage to President Cleveland on June 2, 1886). Prior to the wedding, Rose Cleveland (Grover's sister) served as hostess.

BENJAMIN HARRISON (1889–1893)
Caroline Lavinia Scott Harrison. After Caroline's death on October 25, 1892, her daughter, Mary Harrison McKee, acted as the nation's hostess.

GROVER CLEVELAND (1893–1897)
Frances Folsom Cleveland

WILLIAM MCKINLEY (1897–1901)
Ida Saxton McKinley

THEODORE ROOSEVELT (1901–1909)
Edith Kermit Carow Roosevelt

WILLIAM HOWARD TAFT (1909–1913)
Helen Herron Taft. While Mrs. Taft was recovering from a stroke, her daughter, Helen Taft, and her three sisters filled in.

WOODROW WILSON (1913–1921)
Ellen Louise Axson Wilson was first lady until her death on August 6, 1914. During Ellen's illness and after her death, Margaret Wilson (daughter) and Helen Bones (Woodrow Wilson's cousin) performed hostess duties. Edith Bolling Galt Wilson became first lady after her marriage to President Wilson on December 18, 1915.

WARREN G. HARDING (1921–1923)
Florence Kling Harding

CALVIN COOLIDGE (1923–1929)
Grace Anna Goodhue Coolidge

HERBERT HOOVER (1929–1933)
Lou Henry Hoover

FRANKLIN D. ROOSEVELT (1933–1945)
Anna Eleanor Roosevelt

HARRY S. TRUMAN (1945–1953)
Elizabeth Virginia Wallace Truman

DWIGHT D. EISENHOWER (1953–1961)
Mamie Geneva Doud Eisenhower

JOHN F. KENNEDY (1961–1963)
Jacqueline Lee Bouvier Kennedy

LYNDON B. JOHNSON (1963–1969)
Claudia Alta (Lady Bird) Taylor Johnson

RICHARD M. NIXON (1969–1974)
Patricia Ryan Nixon

GERALD R. FORD (1974–1977)
Elizabeth Bloomer Ford

JIMMY CARTER (1977–1981)
Eleanor Rosalynn Smith Carter

RONALD REAGAN (1981–1989)
Nancy Davis Reagan

GEORGE H.W. BUSH (1989–1993)
Barbara Pierce Bush

WILLIAM J. CLINTON (1993–2001)
Hillary Rodham Clinton

GEORGE W. BUSH (2001–present)
Laura Welch Bush

FURTHER READING

Andersen, Christopher. *George and Laura: Portrait of an American Marriage*. New York: HarperCollins, 2002.

Anthony, Carl Sferrazza. *America's Most Influential First Ladies*. Minneapolis: Oliver Press, Inc., 1996.

———. *First Ladies: The Saga of the Presidents' Wives and Their Power, 1789–1961*. New York: William Morrow & Co., 1990.

———. *First Ladies: The Saga of the Presidents' Wives and Their Power 1961–1990*. New York: William Morrow & Co., 1991.

Boller, Paul F., Jr. *Presidential Wives: An Anecdotal History*. 2d ed. New York: Oxford University Press, 1998.

Bowles, Hamish, ed. *Jacqueline Kennedy: The White House Years: Selections from the John F. Kennedy Library and Museum*. New York: Bulfinch Press, 2001.

Bush, Barbara. *Barbara Bush: A Memoir*. New York: Scribner, 1994.

Carter, Rosalynn. *First Lady from Plains*. Fayetteville, Ark.: University of Arkansas Press, 1996.

Eisenhower, Julie Nixon. *Pat Nixon: The Untold Story*. New York: Simon & Schuster, 1986.

Eisenhower, Susan. *Mrs. Ike: Memories and Reflections on the Life of Mamie Eisenhower.* Dulles, Va.: Capital Books, Inc., 2002.

Felix, Antonia. *Laura: America's First Lady, First Mother.* Avon, Mass.: Adams Media Corporation, 2002.

Goodwin, Doris Kearns. *No Ordinary Time: Franklin and Eleanor Roosevelt: The Home Front in World War II.* New York: Simon & Schuster, 1995.

Marton, Kati. *Hidden Power: Presidential Marriages That Shaped Our History.* New York: Anchor Books, 2002.

Morris, Sylvia Jukes. *Edith Kermit Roosevelt: Portrait of a First Lady.* New York: Random House, 2001.

Taylor, Sherri Peel. *Influential First Ladies (History Makers).* San Diego: Lucent Books, 2001.

Withey, Lynne. *Dearest Friend: The Life of Abigail Adams.* New York: Simon & Schuster, 2002.

PLACES TO VISIT

If you are thinking about visiting any of the places of interest listed below, please call the institutions ahead of time for hours of operation, directions, and specific details about the collections.

ELEANOR ROOSEVELT NATIONAL HISTORIC SITE (VAL-KILL)
Route 9G
Hyde Park, New York
(845) 229-5302
www.nps.gov/elro/home.htm

GEORGE BUSH PRESIDENTIAL LIBRARY AND MUSEUM
1000 George Bush Drive West
College Station, Texas
(979) 691-4000
http://bushlibrary.tamu.edu

GREENSBORO HISTORICAL MUSEUM
130 Summit Avenue
Greensboro, North Carolina
(336) 373-2043
www.greensborohistory.org
Features a Dolley Madison exhibit.

JAMES MADISON'S MONTPELIER
11407 Constitution Highway
Montpelier Station, Virginia 22957
(703) 672-2728
www.montpelier.org
Home of James and Dolley Madison.

JOHN F. KENNEDY LIBRARY AND MUSEUM
Columbia Point
Boston, Massachusetts
(877) 616-4599
www.cs.umb.edu/jfklibrary/

MAMIE DOUD EISENHOWER BIRTHPLACE
709 Carroll Street
Boone, Iowa
(515) 432-1896
www.mamiesbirthplace.homestead.com

MARY TODD LINCOLN HOUSE
578 West Main Street
Lexington, Kentucky
Phone: (606) 233-9999
www.mtlhouse.org

GEORGE WASHINGTON'S MOUNT VERNON ESTATE AND GARDENS
Mount Vernon, Virginia
www.mountvernon.org
(703) 780-2000
Home of George and Martha Washington.

THE NATIONAL FIRST LADIES' LIBRARY
The Saxton McKinley House
311 Market Avenue South
Canton, Ohio
(330) 452-0876
www.firstladies.org

RICHARD NIXON LIBRARY & BIRTHPLACE
18001 Yorba Linda Boulevard
Yorba Linda, California
(714) 993-3393
www.nixonfoundation.org

SMITHSONIAN NATIONAL MUSEUM OF AMERICAN HISTORY
First Ladies Exhibition
14th Street and Constitution Avenue NW
Washington, D.C.
(202) 357-2700 (voice)
(202) 357-1729 (TTY)
www.americanhistory.si.edu
Includes gowns worn by the first ladies.

THE WHITE HOUSE
1600 Pennsylvania Avenue NW
Washington, D.C.
(202) 456-7041
www.whitehouse.gov/history/tours/

PHOTO CREDITS

INDEX